Instructional Guide

for

THE ART OF BEING HUMAN

Second Edition

For the Classroom Instructor

For the Telecourse Instructor

Richard Paul Janaro
Project Director
THE ART OF BEING HUMAN
Miami-Dade Community College

HARPER & ROW, PUBLISHERS, New York
Cambridge, Philadelphia, San Francisco,
London, Mexico City, São Paulo, Sydney

Instructional Guide for The Art of Being Human, Second Edition

ISBN: 0-06-363266-7

TABLE OF CONTENTS

FOREWORD

THE ART OF BEING HUMAN can be a total program--an interdisciplinary, issue-oriented one semester course presenting broad perspectives in the humanities to college students or to members of the community, or it can be a library of resources in the humanities. The modular structure guarantees maximum flexibility. Each module represents a week's work, and none of the modules refers to those which have preceded or will follow (though there are implied connections). Instructors may offer the program as designed, rearrange the order, or substitute topics which better suit their needs.

The existing order, which is reflected in both the textbook and the student study guide, is designed to create a sequence of insights, leading to a synthesis yielded by Module XV, <u>The Humaniites: An Eternal Quest for Form</u>. The issue of form--what the word <u>means</u>, whether it is the same for everyone, and how it relates to taste--struck the course team as being crucial to an understanding of what the humanities are and what they can do for each of us. Life without form, the course hopes to show, is aimless and dull.

The course departs from traditional introductions in that it encourages students to decide for themselves which forms or periods suit their taste. We hope students will reach the conclusion that since nothing is permanent, a close-minded view of <u>any</u> issue would mean a betrayal of one's essential humanity. We do not insist that classical music is "better" than folk, or that Aristotle is more important than Thoreau, or that philosophy is ultimately more valuable than a Zen painting. We view the human adventure as a beautiful, never-ending need to make connections--all manner of them.

To encourage open-mindedness, therefore, we tend to present the material in a "this side/that side" or "yin/yang" way. In other words, we actively seek out alternatives and options. Knowing what the humanities are in general is not enough. One must know what choices are available.

Besides, the principle of alternation, of polarity, precludes the possibility that any course design team may impose one dominant point of view or philosophy upon the student. True, the choices involved in any given module had to be predetermined, but conscientious designers can do no more than set forth matters in the most realistic and honest way they know. The fact that eleven persons were making the decisions also helped to keep esoteric viewpoints out of the deliberations. In any event, since the principle of polarity assumes the importance of argumentation, the instructor may freely take issue with any of the ideas, or sets of choices, and still be faithful to the spirit of humanism, which is, after all, the art of keeping oneself open to life.

So concerned were we that THE ART OF BEING HUMAN would strike responsive chords in participating faculty and students, so open were we in our desire to avoid well-traveled roads, elitism, and the vested interests of specialists, that we decided to subject the entire program to a thorough pilot test before any of the components became widely available. Six faculty members from Miami-Dade Community College volunteered their services and, through a most fortunate chain of circumstances, the Humanities Department of Daytona Beach Community College discovered the course and offered to participate in the testing. All in all, eight instructors and about 300 students were involved in the "sneak preview." Feedback from everyone was eagerly sought and acted upon. As a result, changes were made in some of the TV programs, and many important additions and deletions led to an extensive alteration of both text and student guide. There is little doubt in our mind that THE ART OF BEING HUMAN reflects the incredible range of input from those who gave and those who took the course. (As a matter of fact, the dividing line between them became somewhat fuzzy.)

The results of the pilot test indicated that the course can be highly successful either as a telecourse for the external student who almost never comes to the campus, or as an alternative version of a classroom course in general education humanities.

BACKGROUND OF THE ORIGINAL PILOT TEST, CONDUCTED IN 1978-79

The pilot test of THE ART OF BEING HUMAN, conducted at both Miami-Dade and Daytona Beach Community Colleges, had as its overriding purpose a determination of how the program might work as a general education introduction to the humanities. Both institutions maintain open-door policies, and both have students of highly varied backgrounds and degrees of academic proficiency. While THE ART OF BEING HUMAN was not designed to be a diluted, simplified presentation of the humanities, it carries only the usual prerequisite for such courses--at the most, two semesters of freshman composition. But composition can even be taken simultaneously. Our assumption was that human beings of average or higher intelligence should be able to complete the program successfully, provided they did the reading and viewed the TV tapes diligently.

Both institutions accepted the program as an equivalent to some existing humanities course. Department chairpeople notified their staffs of the experiment, and faculty were assembled on a volunteer basis. Because one requirement was that each faculty member would submit test items and attend regular meetings on the progress of the course, the administrations of both schools provided either release time or overload points. In most cases, faculty chose to have a reduced load instead of extra remuneration.

One condition set forth by the administration of each of Miami-Dade's three campuses participating in the experiment was that the course be shown to fulfill all or nearly all of the minimum learning objectives for the equivalent course. Since it was ascertained that the condition was met, the course team believed that a meaningful comparison could be made between student performance in the pilot test and that evidenced in the equivalent courses.

At Miami-Dade approximately 250 students were enrolled in six sections of the course; average class size was about 40. This number approximates the workable size for standard courses in general education humanities. No attempt was made to "screen" the students, or even to inform them at the time of enrollment that they were being admitted into an experimental section of a new program. The reasoning was this: except for the minimum learning objectives, no two sections of general education humanities are ever exactly alike. There are no departmental texts or examinations. Hence, all students face the same random odds when they enroll in any section of humanities.

At Daytona Beach, however, the course was advertised in advance as THE ART OF BEING HUMAN, and as "Humanities on Television." All potential enrollees were given a brief description of the innovative nature of the program. The average size of the two sections was 20, which, the course team was told, was a little smaller than normal for general education humanities. The size was, however, not *significantly* small.

At organizational meetings between the faculty of both schools it was decided that all sections would read the first 15 chapters of the text, made available in a preliminary offset edition, as well as the entire study guide, and would view all 30 of the videotapes. We agreed that the amount of work might exceed what was required in some sections of humanities, but we saw no point in testing any but a complete program. Even though at the first meeting of the classes students were informed what the reading and viewing loads would be, there was no mass exodus to other sections. As a matter of fact, quite the reverse happened. Most of the faculty noticed a great deal of enthusiasm for the program and what it appeared to promise.

Because of the smaller class sizes at Daytona Beach Community College, the faculty members there decided to coordinate two strongly contrasting approaches to the course. One section met scrupulously three hours per week. Tapes were shown on two of the days, and general discussions of the module were conducted during the third class period. Students in the other sections were asked to view the tapes in the Learning Resources Center at their own convenience, and were given the option of attending in-class discussions. In other words, the second section simulated some of the conditions of the telecourse taken by the external student.

Neither of the Daytona Beach instructors reported poor daily class attendance. Those who did not have to come to class did so because they either enjoyed the discussions or were grateful for the chance to ask questions about the text and the video programs. The course team drew the inescapable conclusion that when THE ART OF BEING HUMAN is offered solely as a telecourse, with few on-campus meetings, some provisions must be made for maintaining ties between instructor and student. It is clearly not a program that should operate autonomously, nor was it our thought that humanists would welcome such a course.

The Miami-Dade instructors reported that their students often complained about not receiving a "fair share" of the instructor's time, especially since all videotape viewing had to take place in the classroom. This meant that the limited time devoted to discussion, and the numbers who might need special attention, created problems that were often frustrating to both faculty and students.

The inescapable conclusion reached here was that when THE ART OF BEING HUMAN is offered as an on-campus classroom course, ample time for discussion must be allowed even if some tapes, or modules, have to be omitted. The issues involved create enormous interest on the students' part, sometimes controversy to the point of heated debate, or even hostility. After all, when you are dealing with matters like love, death, and the question of God's existence, you are bound to find that very fixed and deep-rooted beliefs are being stirred, and perhaps challenged. Students in the classroom will want to voice their objections, or at least to give vent to their feelings on some of the subjects.

One Miami-Dade pilot test instructor recommended that some of the videotapes be omitted in favor of having more time for class discussion. Another took time to meet with groups of students in her office. At Daytona Beach, the instructor who made class attendance optional indicated that oftentimes the discussion on a certain tape continued until late into the afternoon.

The section entitled "A Note to the Telecourse Instructor" contains suggestions for handling the course with external students, who will surely feel somewhat abandoned if they are left entirely on their own without an adequate chance to communicate.

All of the Miami-Dade faculty members reported continual feedback from students, sometimes quite negative. Statements like "We never really finished talking about last week's subject, and here we are facing another one" were frequent, as well as "There is too much material to sort through. It's hard to get ready for the tests." At the same time, nearly all of the students who took the first test were on hand for the final, suggesting that when the _opportunity_ to communicate matches the _need_ to communicate, students tend to remain satisfied with a course.

At Daytona Beach, where the smaller classes allowed for considerable expression of student thought and feeling, instructors reported a rather continuous flow of protest, agreement, or disagreement, and suggestions for improvement, either in the print material or the videotapes. "I didn't understand this" and "How can they say that?" were common remarks.

The Project Director of the program and the authors of both the text and study guide kept in constant touch with the feedback; alterations were made, much in the manner of a play's out-of-town tryouts.

One videotape was completely redone, from script to production. Substantial changes were made in several others. Both text and study guide, however, most profoundly reflect the suggestions from teachers and students alike. There must surely be very few courses in which print support owes so much to input from those actively participating in the program.

RESULTS OF THE ORIGINAL PILOT TEST

Examination scores and final grades do not a course make, nor do they necessarily represent comments on or solutions to the problems a course may have. Everyone knows that although 90% of the students enrolled in a course may achieve a grade of "A," the course could well have been a hideous bore, or an insult to the participants' intelligence. It could also have been so stimulating and exciting that the participants put forth a phenomenal effort.

For this reason, the course team was not concerned only about final grades as such. We were interested, rather, in getting the whole picture, which we divided into the following components:

1. minimum performance requirements
2. the examination questions
3. the amount of work required
4. the readability and usefulness of the text
5. the quality and usefulness of the videotapes
6. the quality and usefulness of the classroom instruction
7. the quality and usefulness of classroom discussions
8. the average daily attendance in this course relative to that in equivalent humanities courses
9. attrition and overall performance relative to those in equivalent humanities courses

MINIMUM PERFORMANCE REQUIREMENTS

In a course as flexible as THE ART OF BEING HUMAN it is impossible to create a set of minimum performance requirements that work in all instances. Each institution must decide what it wants from participating students. After conducting an all-day preliminary meeting at Daytona Beach, Florida, the pilot test faculty decided upon the following requirements:

1. The student had to pass three one-hour examinations with a satisfactory score.
2. The examinations would consist of both multiple-choice and short-answer essay questions.
3. The multiple-choice items would measure the student's cognitive growth from reading the text and study guide.
4. The short-answer essay questions would allow the student to express affective reactions to the videotapes.
5. There would be a fourth, or comprehensive, examination offered at the discretion of the instructor as an option for students who wanted the chance to improve their over-all class standing.
6. Participants could enhance their grades by attending theaters, art galleries, and concerts and submitting reviews of these events.

The first examination covered Modules I through IV, and consisted of twenty-five multiple-choice items and five short-answer essay questions. On the objective section of the test, the mean score was 13.29 and the reliability index was .77. This second figure tells us whether a test is adequately tapping the resources of the good student. As you can see, the index, while respectable, was not a matter for rejoicing. Nor did we believe that a mean score of just over 50% was unimprovable.

When canvassed, the majority of students indicated they would have preferred more multiple-choice items. A testing specialist, assigned to Miami-Dade to work with the pilot test faculty, concurred in this view, adding that both mean scores and reliability indexes tend to rise as the number of test items increases.

What "saved" the students was the generally higher score each one achieved on the essay section of the examination. Since there were no clearcut right and wrong answers, the student was rewarded with points so long as he or she demonstrated genuine involvement with the videotapes. It was decided to expand the multiple-choice section to 50 questions, while retaining the essay section.

Examination II, which covered Modules V through X, saw better results. The reliability index jumped to .90, while the mean score of the objective section of the test was 28.62 out of a possible 50. Even more important, perhaps, scores on individual items showed that, with a few exceptions, the options were well enough balanced so that the good students were able to discern the correct response, while the ill-prepared students had difficulty guessing their way through the test. Overall, far fewer students complained about Examination II.

At the conclusion of the first test, instructors announced to their classes that no decision had yet been reached relative to the curving of grades. (If you prefer the technical distinction, we had not decided whether to use norm-referencing, which would curve the grades, or criterion-referencing, which would establish absolute minimal scores for every grade.) After Examination II, the pilot test faculty agreed upon norm-referencing by section in view of the highly divergent backgrounds of the students. (Criterion referencers, by the way, do not agree that norm-referencing by sections makes sense in an open-door institution.)

Examination III, covering Modules XI through XV, brought a mean score of 31.55[1] out of a possible 50, and a reliability index of .88. By this time, most students had apparently found the formula for making the course work. They seemed to be reading and viewing more diligently. Moreover, the norm-referencing was very much to their liking, and seemed to reduce the threat the course had posed for some at the beginning.

Because so many had made low scores on Examination I, the entire pilot faculty voted to offer the optional fourth, or comprehensive, examination. Those who were satisfied with the grade they were making could go home a day early. Those who wanted a substitute for their poorest grade or a make-up test, or who hoped to improve their grade,

---

[1] This is, of course, the raw mean score, and acquired a different significance in each section.

could take the examination if they wished. Like the others, the comprehensive had 50 multiple-choice items, but there were no essay questions. For the first time in the course, affective responses were handled through multiple-choice, a situation which created some problems. But the course team believes it learned a great deal from the experiment. The current student guide contains both cognitive and affective multiple-choice items representative of the kind of questions which had some success with the students in the pilot test.

EXAMINATION QUESTIONS

While overall numerical scores in the four examinations compared favorably with overall numerical scores achieved in objective tests by students in equivalent courses, the pilot faculty and the course design team studied the computer breakdown of student performances on each item of each test. In this way, poor questions were discarded. A poor question is one which is either too easy, indicating that the incorrect responses are not challenging and do not seriously discriminate between those who are and those who are not prepared, or too difficult or ambiguous, so that the generally high-scoring student is hard put to discern the supposedly correct response. A predominance of such questions creates a low overall reliability index. As we have seen, the pilot test examinations tended to be quite reliable; therefore, we may conclude that most of the items worked.

On the other hand, this fact alone does not guarantee that the best possible selection of items was made, or that the students were given the best opportunities to demonstrate what they had absorbed. In their feedback the students, especially in the large classes, complained that even though the examination questions often appeared fair _in retrospect_, they had felt threatened before each test because of the broad spectrum of possible questions that kept occurring to them. The larger classes also indicated that it was harder to prepare for an issue-oriented test than one which covered specific segments of historical time.

The pilot test edition of the study guide did not contain the surveys found in the present version. These, we feel confident, will prove very helpful, especially to the external student or to large classes.

Several of the pilot test faculty distributed essay question topics prior to each examination, and told their classes that five of the topics would appear on the actual test. The generally better performances were attributed to the lessening of student apprehension. In no case did a faculty member "teach to" the objective portion of an examination, since the final selection of questions was made by the chairperson of the course team and a testing consultant.

The moral is _to be very clear about the sort of thing the students can be expected to demonstrate on tests, and to make certain that tests actually do reflect the approach taken by the instructor. It would be most unwise, considering the flexibility of the program, to compose_ examinations at the last minute without having made a strong point of what students should emphasize in their preparations.

If the course is taught as an honors program or in small classes, with ample opportunity for discussions, then examinations can even be discarded in favor of the Journal, suggested topics for which are provided in the module discussions.

AMOUNT OF WORK REQUIRED

The text contains 16 chapters, 15 of which were assigned to all participating classes. The chapter now called "On Being a Critical Thinker" was optional, although in the opinion of the course team it contains important material and should be read, at least in part. (Some of the instructors who taught the course on their own the semester following that of the pilot test reported excellent class response to this chapter.)

In addition, the students were told to read the appropriate chapter in the study guide, and to be responsible for viewing the weekly tapes, either in class or in learning centers located in audio-visual departments.

Seventy percent of the students polled at the conclusion of the course indicated that the amount of reading and viewing was excessive, or at least more than they were accustomed to in general education courses

It should be pointed out, however, that at Daytona Beach Community College, where the two small classes were located, students generally did not feel that they had been overworked. It is quite possible that the sense of having a great deal to cover may correlate with the size of a class, and the lack of time that can be given to the individual student. It may be closely related to the apprehension experienced by the students in the larger groups before each examination.

Here are some suggestions from the course team:

1. If classes are very large and opportunities for extended discussions will be limited, some sections can be skipped in some of the text chapters at the discretion of the instructor or participating faculties.

2. In classroom courses as a whole, a number of videotapes could be omitted in favor of more discussion time. Since all 30 tapes seemed necessary to the overall design, the course team naturally is reluctant to make recommendations on this score. Individual instructors or participating faculties will need to make their own decisions relative to the emphasis to be given and the examination questions to be used.

3. Since 75% of the students polled indicated that the videotapes were either very helpful or helpful, compared to 81% who said the same of the text, one would be advised to rely on reading to a greater extent than viewing, if a choice must be made. Obviously, in the telecourses the balance between the two should be maintained.

4. The study guide has been thoroughly revised since the pilot test. It is shorter, the overviews are more cogent, and a Check List of Main Ideas is now provided for each unit. Students should be encouraged to read this material very carefully. The guide should substantially reduce the sort of concerns expressed by pilot test participants and, because it clearly focuses on the major themes running through the course, it should help to justify the amount of work assigned.

THE TEXT

As already mentioned, students tended to rely on the text quite strongly. But it should not be thought that the text exactly parallels the videotapes. They were developed cooperatively, it is true, but the book was also designed to stand alone as an alternate means of presenting the humanities to college students. In some institutions the text will be used independently of the video programs. This means that the instructor will not find a point-by-point correspondence between text chapters and video programs, though a great deal of parallelism exists.

The fact that students in the pilot test expressed concern over impending examinations can be partly attributed to the lack of the Surveys now included in the study guide. Clarity in the presentation of the text material will, however, be just as important as the Surveys themselves. In other words, instructors who are not following the program as presented in the study guide need to outline their main points and find those portions of the text which are relevant to them.

The pilot test indicated the importance of having a tight teaching package in advance. It is for this reason that the present structure, outlined in the study guide, now exists.

Student evaluations reported that on the whole the text seemed quite readable. The fact that many points were made through references to the contemporary scene was regarded as a plus. Students also seemed to enjoy the magazine-type format, with boxed material in the margins.

This material is of three varieties: relevant quotations from other sources; important quotations from the text itself, which highlight major points; and running summaries or paraphrasing of whole sections. The instructor should point out at the beginning of the course that marginal boxes offer an excellent method of reviewing for examinations.

THE VIDEOTAPES

Since the pilot test was conducted strictly as a classroom program, and since all 30 videotapes were shown, it was not surprising to discover that students had trouble absorbing all of the material contained in the tapes. Some generalizations about these tapes and their function in the program can be made:

1. The tapes are mainly affective in their approach. With a few exceptions, they do not contain on-camera hosts making direct points. In many instances they deal with the issue through a narrative. It is what happens to characters that informs the viewer of the underlying meaning.

2. The tapes are designed as organic components of the entire program. They should be dealt with as if they were films rented as visual support for the curriculum. Almost every one of the tapes can stand alone outside the context of the module in which it appears. Within the context of the module it offers creative support for instructor or text. The tapes amplify the themes of the modules in many ways.

3. It is the "hunch" of the course team that visual experience, when it is stimulating and provocative, does more for students than can be directly measured through tests and even journals. Many of the tapes may leave residuals--kernels of ideas that won't burst open for months, perhaps years. The students ought to be advised of this possibility.

They can even be told that they may not understand everything about every tape upon first viewing, but may look back later on this or that incident and suddenly say "So that's what it meant!"

4. Students polled were quite positive about the essay question method of responding to the tapes. The course team recommends that the practice be continued wherever and as often as feasible.

   Even in telecourses with large enrollments, students will have to come to the campus at least twice, preferably three times, a semester for examinations. While these will be mostly computer graded, a number of short answer essay items should not tax the supervising faculty members.

5. On the other hand, the tapes undoubtedly contain a good deal of cognitive information that faculty may well expect students to have absorbed. In the Course Information brochure or welcome letter that participating institutions or instructors may want to prepare, the rules for viewing the tapes should be clearly stated.

   Note-taking during the viewing process needs to be kept to a minimum. After all, nobody (except perhaps a critic) takes a notepad to a movie or watches TV at home with a pencil in one hand. Major cognitive points tend to announce themselves boldly, and students who view the tapes with a reasonable degree of concentration can be assured that they will retain the information they will need.

   As for the essay items, students can be told that a wide range of attitudes and feelings is possible, but that their responses must reflect a sincere involvement with the tape in question.

   Not one student complained that a pilot test instructor's evaluation of an essay response was unfair. In nearly every instance involving partial or no credit for an answer, it seemed evident that the tape had not been seen at all, that the student's thinking was cloudy, or that there was a real writing problem, usually quite familiar to the student by now.

6. Some evidence exists to support the belief that a strong visual component in a course, even affectively oriented, can have carry-over to cognitive areas, especially the ability to think straight. One reason may be a relaxation in the cognitive "section" of the brain. Forced concentration, especially when one is in no mood for it, often results in the tortured logic and vagueness with which writing teachers are familiar.

   Where this program is offered as a classroom course, instructors might well consider using tapes as a lead-in for an immediate writing assignment. (Topics for such assignments are provided in the module-by-module coverage later in the manual.)

7. In most cases, a relationship exists between the two tapes in a module, even though each one can stand alone. One module, for example, has one tape on Apollo, the other on Dionysus. In another, the first tape explicates tragedy, the second, comedy. Both of these examples involve an actual balance, where two contrasting conditions or experiences need to coexist within human awareness.

   In preparing to teach the course, the instructor should consider possible relationships between the tapes--assuming that both will be used, of course--and make certain the students are aware of them.

   The strength of the relationship (as in Apollo and Dionysus) may well be used to determine in which modules pairs of tapes need to be shown.

CLASSROOM INSTRUCTION

Students in the pilot test program tended to appreciate their classroom instructor. Most indicated they probably would have had some trouble with the course had it not been for the guidance provided. This attitude supported the view that, because of the amount of time devoted to tape-viewing, there was often insufficient discussion of important points.

With the revised study guide in hand, the conscientious external student should be able to steer himself through the program. In the classroom course, however, a different relationship between student and material occurs with the teacher as catalyst. It can become a very different program, but one equally as valid.

The classroom instructor may take issue with ideas, statements, or interpretations. It should be made clear at the outset that both text and videotapes represent points of departure. The classroom instructor becomes a course component, introducing original perspectives wherever desirable.

While the pilot test faculty agreed to administer program-wide examinations, some of them gave weekly quizzes on what had transpired in class. In this way, some of their own input was reflected. As the program is utilized in varying settings, it can become deeply personalized to suit the needs of a given classroom instructor. When this happens, the student deserves to be told how much of the total learning experience will depend upon the text, how much on the tapes, and how much on the instructor's lectures.

CLASSROOM DISCUSSIONS OR DISCUSSION GROUPS

As we have seen, THE ART OF BEING HUMAN invites discussion--so much so that some of the pilot test instructors indicated they either did continue, or could have continued the class meeting for several hours. Obviously the need students have for expressing themselves on many of the issues raised was anticipated by the course team. The opportunity for discussion can well be built into the evaluative mechanism of the program.

Students in classroom courses can be informed at the outset that participation in discussion groups can be organized on a semester-long basis. Specific tasks can be given at the beginning of a discussion period with the group leader asked to submit a summary of what the group generally said, either orally or in writing. Some pilot test instructors had great success using audiocassettes and spot-checking them to make certain all participants contributed something to the discussion. Discussion topics can be taken from the teaching outlines provided for the individual modules.

ATTENDANCE

All institutions engage in research on classroom attendance. There are figures for general education courses, vocational courses, and courses in a major subject. Attendance varies with the time of the day or night, the season of the year, and both the popularity and effectiveness of a given instructor. There are, in fact, so many variables that definitive conclusions are difficult to make relative to average daily attendance for the pilot test program.

One instructor reported that attendance in the pilot test course was definitely not as good as that for equivalent courses he was also teaching. Others reported better than average attendance. There was some correlation observed between test performances, overall final grades, and average daily attendance. It's advisable to stress to both telecourse and classroom students the importance of finding out what is going on at all times. Information on where and when tapes can be viewed by individual students should be made readily available, and students should be reminded of the need to stay caught up on their reading. One instructor, who gave short weekly quizzes, reported 100% attendance each day.

For the external student, telephone hotlines should be accessible at widely publicized times of the day or week. Commitments to answer the phones should be scrupulously kept. An ongoing snag in television education is the loss of contact between student and campus. With the amount of material in THE ART OF BEING HUMAN, such a loss could be disheartening indeed.

"Attendance" in a telecourse is ultimately measured by attrition. Students who fall behind, or who try to see all of the tapes and read the whole text the week before the final, can fall by the wayside. There is a certain rhythm to taking a telecourse, and an introductory on-campus seminar, to be discussed, should be offered to help the students find it.

ATTRITION AND OVERALL PERFORMANCE

THE ART OF BEING HUMAN pilot test faculty lost only 15 students from the first to the final examination; however, the total attrition was around 30%, a figure not inconsistent with general education statistics gathered in community colleges around the country. Like attendance, attrition can be analyzed from the standpoint of many variables, but it is fairly safe in this instance to say that neither the course itself nor the quality of instruction could have been largely responsible for the loss of students. In other words, the students who took the first test generally stayed with the course until the end, *even if the first grade was very low*.

General education teachers, especially in urban institutions, are familiar with the pattern. A significant number of students will sign up for a course and never show up for even one class. Often a drop in attendance can be noted from the first to the second week, so that at the time of the first examination one is teaching a relatively constant group, which can be as much as 40% smaller than the original enrollment figure indicated. Those who have disappeared never really got their feet wet, and this cannot be interpreted as a genuinely negative response.

True, some students wander away at the beginning because a course sounds as if it is not for them. Perhaps some of the pilot test instructors made too much of the non-traditional nature of the course, or the fact that this was an untried program. At all events, we can profit from the one really significant attrition factor--the drop from original enrollment to first test--and make some generalizations:

1. The course seems to have abundant strength, so that there is no need to make it sound suspiciously experimental. It is not, in fact, very experimental. It is rooted in basic human psychology. Students should be told that the course is really for and about them.

2. It is wiser to open up on a positive rather than a negative note. Instructors should talk about what the course is and does, and what is expected of the students, not about how the course differs from so-called "traditional" courses. In most cases, students have not taken the other courses, so they cannot make a comparison.

3. If the program is offered as an on-campus classroom course, the role of the video component should be clarified at the outset. General education students often become discouraged at the thought of so much video, for in their past experience they will no doubt have watched a great deal of television that really was a substitute for a teacher, and they have become understandably scornful of the medium.

4. In the classroom, a proper introduction to each tape is desirable. Human contact should made at the beginning of the class hour, and the tape fitted into an identifiable context.

5. Since telecourse attrition rates tend to be very high anyway, a contact method needs to be devised and consistently utilized. For this reason, suggested responses to the study guide Surveys are contained in this manual. All students should be encouraged to mail or hand in these Surveys, and some form of feedback should be provided. Letters

can be sent out to students not answering the Survey questions, written in a tone that suggests all is not lost.

6. One very good reason for encouraging students to stay with the program is that it does seem to have a positive and beneficial effect on those who do. After all, it was designed to be helpful to people.

If final grades serve as an index to the overall performance of a student in a course, then we may say there were a number of outstanding performances in the pilot test. The instructors, as we pointed out, norm-referenced their grades, but only after discussing the matter with their classes and asking for recommendations. The majority of students voted for the curve, saying they did not want to be competing against people in other sections, and even in other cities. The course team, reviewing the grade distribution, could only conclude that norm-referencing produced what norm-referencing always does--a bell curve. Many educators, of course, point to the cynical implications of the bell curve, and the assumption at the outset that some people are going to fail. True, the low grades were indeed low enough to justify failure, and some purists might not have approved of someone's passing with a numerical average of 60. But general education courses in community colleges always have these problems. THE ART OF BEING HUMAN neither solved all the problems nor created significant new ones.

What is probably most important to remember is the high retention of students from the first examination to the final, and the low, very low, last-minute dropout rate. This indicates that for the typical community college student the program seemed to have worked quite well.

Students were invited to make additional comments on the backs of the evaluation forms. A very high percentage of those who took the trouble to write something (around 50% of the total enrollment) were very high in their praise of the course. A minority were vehement in their disapproval of the course, mainly on these grounds: the length of the reading assignments, the amount of TV viewing involved, and the fact that they hadn't learned much from most of the programs.

Students who did well throughout the course seemed uniform in their view that they had been challenged and stimulated, and six of the eight participating faculty indicated that the experience had been a profound one for them. One instructor said that her life had been completely altered, not necessarily by the material itself, but by the fact that she had been forced to confront some issues she had tended to avoid.

A NOTE TO THE TELECOURSE INSTRUCTOR

THE ART OF BEING HUMAN was designed as a telecourse. If you read the analysis of the pilot test, you no doubt saw that students frequently complained about the amount of material covered and the lack of time for discussion. But it must be said here that these complaints were made by students who <u>had</u> the opportunity for <u>some</u> discussion. Even the experimental section, in which students were to view the tapes on their own and then come or not come to class as they wished, offered the option of classroom discussion. As you look through the instructional guide, you will see an abundance of discussion topics, any one of which would set off a lengthy exchange between students and instructors.

On the other hand, students who enroll in the telecourse will have no expectation of such exchanges. The study guide will focus their attention on the major points in each module, while the survey questions will help prepare them for the examinations. Without classroom discussion something is lost, yes. But an advantage of the telecourse is that the material is more readily fixed in the mind.

However, contact between the remote setting and the campus must be maintained. You should indicate your office hours and telephone number, and display these prominently in the registration materials. You should always be there at the phone or arrange to have someone else in your place--someone who is quite familiar with the program.

Where possible, arrangements should be made with local radio stations for an open-phone broadcast at least once a week. This kind of communication has been successfully used by many institutions offering courses through television.

If you use a computer to communicate the survey prescriptions provided in this manual, you should add a personal letter with each turnaround. The computer can be programmed to tell the student whether his or her grade has gone up or down each time, and to add a note of encouragement. You may also want to have the computer send letters to those who are not mailing in the surveys, suggesting that they start doing so.

Most telecourses hold two to three on-campus examinations. For this program three exams would seem to be an absolute minimum, perhaps after Modules IV, X, and XV. The first test should be given no later than a month into the course. After the first test, nearly all the students in the pilot seemed to relax and enjoy themselves.

If the size of the enrollment permits, you should include some short answer essay questions on each exam. In the pilot test these proved to be the best way of determining what the students had absorbed from the videotapes; and the essay points helped to pull scores up.

Should you decide to use Goals 7 and 8, which are listed in the study guide, you should prepare and then distribute guidelines for reviewing local events in theater, film, music, and art. The reviews can be used to offset other grades, for extra credit, or as integral components of a contractual grading system. These guidelines should be detailed, so that students need not feel bewildered at the prospect of having to put into words what they have experienced.

A Recommended Opening Workshop

Even if the size of the enrollment is too large to make personal contact all but impossible throughout the semester, you should try to hold an introductory workshop on campus for all persons registered prior to the first telecast. At least half a day should be allowed.

With a large group, you can subdivide into smaller units, using zodiac signs or simply numbers handed out to each person upon arrival. After spending some time exchanging names and discussing reasons for taking a telecourse, the members of each group can be given certain questions to answer. Examples:

1. What is a humanist?
2. What are the humanities?
3. What are the local humanistic resources?
4. How much national support should the humanities receive?
5. How important are the humanities relative to nuclear disarmament, energy, inflation, etc.?
6. What is freedom?
7. What is happiness?

You have the idea. Any of the major issues in the course can be used for discussion. The sharing session afterward will help set the course up for the students. If the group is not large, hold an open forum. Talk about:

1. Study habits
2. Viewing the tapes
3. Mailing in the Surveys
4. Extra credit reviews
5. Phoning you

Human relations exercises can also be effective, especially if you have the assistance of counselors or school psychologists trained in the methodology. These are appropriate for this course, since one of the major themes of the course is opening one's heart and mind to what others believe and feel.

The on-campus workshop will not only start everyone off on the right foot, but it can lead to higher enrollment if this should prove feasible.

A NOTE ON THE REVISION OF TEXT AND TELECOURSE

In 1980 THE ART OF BEING HUMAN became available nationally as a complete package: 30 half-hour television programs; a text; a student study guide; and an instructor's manual. Having gone through the extensive pilot testing described on the preceding pages, and a number of significant revisions deemed necessary from the feedback received, the course proved viable as televised education for the external student and as a classroom experience for the on-campus general education student. In fact, THE ART OF BEING HUMAN during the past three years has divided itself almost equally between the campus and the living room. The text has been in use in over two hundred institutions, both community and four-year colleges. It has been used in humanities, English and, here and there, psychology courses. The telecourse has been shown several times through the adult education division of the Public Broadcasting Service.

The very fact that the text is now in its Second Edition indicates at least a modest degree of "interest," whatever that nebulous term may be taken to mean. Or that the television programs have been in wide circulation. Or that letters have come in from readers and viewers in numerous walks of life, representing a wide variety of age and interest levels--from a dedicated Buddhist practitioner in California, who objected to the narrator's voice drowning out the words of a Zen Master being interviewed, to a member of an American Indian tribe in northern Minnesota, who castigated us in no uncertain terms for omitting Indian literature and mythology from the text. There have been many favorable responses, to be sure. But with the assurance that interest was there, and that many improvements could be made in both the course and the text, we set about the task of revising the original product.

The first step was to restructure the telecourse. The original Module II ("Man, the Esthetic Being") for example was, as many voices made evident, too complex and difficult for its placement during the second week of study. Its title was also offensive to a good many, who made us see that the generic term "man" was no longer an appropriate designation for the human race.

A more pointedly humanistic orientation seemed also desirable. The psychological benefits of using the humanities as personal resources would still underlie the entire program, but the humanistic disciplines needed to be kept in the forefront so that students would never lose sight of the fact that they are studying the nature of human thought and creativity, and how these can enhance our lives. The major themes about which the humanities concern themselves would be treated just as that--themes in the humanities, not major life issues which can also be found in the humanities.

In short, the purpose of revising the telecourse was to crystallize its integrity as an introduction to the humanities and to minimize its sometimes ambiguous existence as a humanities/psychology course. The authors of the text and the telecourse team still believe that the two areas overlap a great deal, as they do in the absolute necessity of relating contemporary scientific advances like quantum theory to the humanities; but they agree that the teaching of THE ART OF BEING HUMAN becomes much more feasible when it crosses disciplines less evidently than it did before.

At the same time, there has been no radical denial of the original premise--namely, that the humanities can no longer be taught as a chronology of Western civilization, or as the cumulative achievement of a few notable individuals (mainly men). The thrust of the course remains what it has always been--the personal meaning of the humanities to the student.

STRUCTURAL POSSIBILITIES

The instructor or faculty starting out to adapt the program to a particular set of needs incurs no obligation to present the material in the order described in the text and the study guide. Since both were developed cooperatively, but not necessarily concurrently, they have parallel linear arrangements. It cannot be denied that the course team saw some advantage to the arrangement, and suggested that it be mentioned here. We have no doubt, however, that as the program is presented to students a number of alterations will take place. It would not be a humanistic offering if this could not happen.

No module refers directly to another, but in its present form, the program could have a cumulative effect. In free-exchange sessions held in some of the pilot classes, there was some indication that it had, though most students were not able to state in so many words just what _total_ experience they had undergone, or what the whole thing had "come to" by the time the final program credits began to roll. Incidentally, there is no good reason that students should be required to have this information readily available. Who knows but that it may take years for many of the insights to make their way into the conscious awareness? The humanities are not exact sciences.

The following is a restatement of the list of modules as they appear in the study guide, with a brief description of what the course team believes each one contributes toward a cumulative experience.

I. "The Essence of Being Human"

On the one hand, there is no such thing--on the other, the human essence is the need to grow, balanced by the willingness to do so. Humans have discovered ways of holding fast to things and resisting change. A major theme in this course is going to be openness to life.

II. "Art and the Artist"

Openness to life can begin when one shows a willingness to investigate the unfamiliar in the humanities, and what better place to experiment than with the visual arts? The student often comes to us with an expectation that art must depict something, either with fidelity to what is "real," or at least with a clearly definable intention on the part of the artist. Here we learn that art of all periods and cultures has one thing in common--imitation, sometimes of the appearance of nature, and sometimes of nature's urge to create new things.

III. "Music: the Planned Environment"

As in art, the unfamiliar in music can be strongly rejected in favor of the "comforting" sounds of the student's everyday experiences. Here, the student is introduced to the idea that as the artificially created audio environment (as opposed to the random, chaotic, often grating sounds which assail our ears) music in its wondrous varieties and its complex interweaving of elements offers us not only a refuge, but ultimately, as we examine our tastes, insights into our own natures. The idea is to be expansive in those tastes, and also in the character we develop.

IV. "Philosophy: Moral Values"

Openness to life, the willingness to grow, an insistence upon one's own identity and the right to create one's personal environment--all these conditions within the human spirit can result in a tremendous unfolding of potential. But there is a limit to the amount of unfolding that can take place before one begins to impinge upon the right of another to grow. Human beings live in social groups, and groups inevitably need moral laws in order to maintain themselves. Hence, the moral dimension of human experience is a crucial area of concern. Question: Where do moral values come from? Who decides? Has anyone the right to create a personal moral code?

V. "Philosophy: Faith and Science"

For centuries religious faith and a scientific approach to the attainment of truth have been in conflict, and have not been viewed as matters of serious choice to intelligent persons. If one chose faith, then science had to be regarded as spurious, offering a false (because only partial) view of the world and humanity's place within it. If one chose science, religion was clearly not a compatible path. This module traces the dazzling forays of contemporary science into ever more mystifying corners of the universe, and the gradual narrowing of the gap between once hostile forces. Today's enlightened citizens have not only a serious choice, but need to be open-minded, once having chosen.

VI. "Philosophy: Eastern/Western Consciousness"

Growth depends upon the cross-fertilization of cultures. It is a step in the right direction for one to learn the ways of another culture. It is growth for one to be willing to empathize with, even participate in, some aspects of that culture. Many Westerners are looking eastward for alternate modes of being, and are developing a synthesis of East and West as a means of making their lives more radiant.

VII. "Drama: Comic and Tragic

A long time ago the theater offered just two kinds of experience: tragic and comic. Despite the proliferation of dramatic genres through the ages, tragedy and comedy remain meaningful polar opposites, not only in the theater itself, but within the human personality. People who would remain open to experience should investigate both poles, and not deny themselves the resources of either as ways of coping with life's less than perfect moments.

VIII. "How the Medium Affects the Message"

The development of each person is strongly influenced by media--those which communicate messages to us from the outside, and the five senses which receive, absorb, and digest those messages. The person whose growth is inhibited is the one who makes too great an investment in a limited number of media without exploring the message potential of the others, e.g., watching television, but not reading; going to movies, but never plays; and thinking reality is essentially what the eye sees.

IX. "Themes in the Humanities: Myth"

While the humanities, because of their variety and the many perspectives they offer, encourage personal growth, we must now consider the fact that humanity also has a tendency to resist growth. If open-mindedness is an ideal, the need for clear certainty is a reality; and once such certainty is achieved, especially through cultural tradition, people can hold on for dear life. Mythology represents just such a cultural tradition, and in this module we study the archetypal certainties we derive from it. Perhaps we are saying here that perpetual open-mindedness may not after all be a blessing--that the time comes when we want to pull the universe tightly around us, and experience the inner comfort of knowing "how things are."

X. "Themes in the Humanities: Love"

Close-mindedness about love can be a source of genuine misery for hosts of people, however. One reason is that love is often viewed as a particular kind of experience, one that is universally sought after, rather than as a myth in itself, with characteristics that change from one period in history to another, from one culture to another, from one individual to another. This module examines the choices offered us in the name of love, and should help us to understand better the confusions we experience, especially when "the other" has made a different choice, or is operating under a different set of rules. In particular, we study certain models derived from the mass media.

XI. "Themes in the Humanities: Happiness"

For many, happiness is the true aim of human life. No less an authority than Aristotle agreed on that much. But no consensus definition of happiness can be found. If we accept the fact that we need to keep searching for a definition, and not limit our view of happiness to a sine qua non, then we may find ourselves much closer than we think. Big questions: Does happiness depend on pleasure? Are pleasure and happiness one and the same? Is it possible to be poor, without status and power, and unrecognized for an achievement, and still be happy?

XII. "Themes in the Humanities: Coping with Death"

A recent book by Elisabeth Kübler-Ross is _Death: The Final Stage of Growth_. For most people, the fact of life's inevitable termination is the inescapable horror, the one unacceptable thing about being human. It is obvious, then, that resources for a more positive attitude toward death must be found; otherwise everything else we may accomplish can go for naught.

XIII. "Themes in the Humanities: Apollo and Dionysus"

We are beginning to see that human growth does not occur straight up, like Jack's beanstalk. It has to be retarded as intensely as it has to be advanced. One reason is surely that the human organism is made up of biological and neurological systems, and the business of a system is to keep itself intact. Both the human mind and human society are driven by principles of systematizing, of making things fit, even as they must, if growth is to occur, desystematize at the right time. People must give up outmoded ideas, and organizations must reorganize from time to time. Apollo and Dionysus represent the two ends of the human spectrum--from the extremes of order to the extremes of disruption. Each person must find a balance within these extremes.

XIV. "Themes in the Humanities: The Meaning of Freedom"

Yes, the humanities encourage open-mindedness, which _seems_ to be a free choice among significant options.

But are we indeed free? What does freedom even mean? This module cannot hope to decide such a complex question once and for all, but it does look at some contrasting views, notably those of the determinists, who say that everything we do (and even feel) is dictated by a previous cause; and the libertarians, who say that free will is indeed a viable concept. Strong focus is on the behaviorism of Skinner and some alternatives from the humanists.

XV. "The Humanities: An Eternal Quest for Form"

Though it does not purport to be a summing up of the entire course, the final module can be presented as a kind of climax to the preceding fourteen weeks. While we have been presenting this view, countered by that objection, while we have been encouraging the students to leave themselves open to possibilities, we see that what we have been basically talking about all along is form. Humanity is a form-seeking species, struggling to achieve arrangements of thoughts, feelings, colors, lines, sounds, words--forms in our private lives, in society, in the arts. And humanity is also a form-destroying species, never satisfied for long with only certain kinds of forms. Of course, we build up traditions, preserving some forms and discarding others--but the coming of age for each of us is the realization that we have the power to add new forms of our own.

MODULE I

THE ESSENCE OF BEING HUMAN

TEACHING OVERVIEW

The very first video program, as the telecourse is designed to be, is _The Man with No Time for Beauty_. Students have enjoyed this program very much, and it is still recommended as the course overture. For one thing, the character of Woodrow Tatlock, the retired widower who travels throughout Europe on a student tour and remains almost totally unaffected by what he sees, seems to be one who strikes a familiar note. Woodrow is widely known, it would appear. Without adopting a patronizing attitude toward Woodrow, the program asks the viewer two serious questions: (1) "What is life like for someone with no background in the humanities?" and (2) "Is this what all of us want?" The program touches upon many questions that will be asked throughout the course, including that of whether standards of beauty are universal. Another question is whether it is okay to have no time for beauty. Students have shown a keen interest in discussing this program, for Woodrow Tatlock raises some of the anti-humanities objections with which many enter a course such as this.

The Way of the Humanist, the companion program, should not be omitted during this first week. It is the positive complement to Woodrow Tatlock. It informs the student of what the humanities _are_, and what they can do for people. As Woodrow represents the pitiable life, devoid of the humanities, the girl mime in the film represents a life enriched by those very resources. The narrator keeps saying "I discovered that being human meant . . ." The door is thus opened for a discussion of what being human can mean, and why it is an art, not a natural skill.

It is recommended, however, that the first week not be spent in excessive discussion of the two programs. Their points are easily made, and it is not necessary to belabor them. Rather, students seem to appreciate some getting-down-to-business. What is going to happen to them in this course? How will they be graded? How may they earn extra points, etc.? Many instructors have indicated that, since the TV programs are for the most part directed toward the affective domain, the setting up of the course should be heavily cognitive in nature.

During the pilot test, some instructors began experimentally, showed the first program, and allowed discussions to go where they might. They reported, however, a certain shyness on the students' part, perhaps induced by some initial confusion about where the course was going, and what was expected of them. Warning: One can be lulled into complacency by the promise of student growth that the course may seem to hold. It is far wiser to let the students know at once that a reading and testing schedule has been established, and that you will be looking for a certain kind of performance from them.

CHECK LISTS OF POINTS OR DISCUSSION TOPICS FROM TEXT

(This list includes Chapters One _and_ Two)

1. The difference between being a human being and practicing the art of being human.

2. What does it mean to say of a person that he or she died "without ever having lived"?

3. Woodrow Tatlock, the man with no time for beauty, as a pervasive human type. He must be dealt with compassionately, and what do we say to the sure-to-be-raised question of "What's wrong with being Woodrow"?

4. The "new" humanism (though it is all there in Matthew Arnold) supports these characteristics: democratic vision; concern for the present; awareness of self; curiosity about technology; universal perspective.

5. Wherever one's humanism leads, the starting place must be the determination to become a critical thinker--one who examines issues fairly and objectively, delaying positive conclusions for as long as possible.

6. We can do much more with our minds than we realize. Scientists, in fact, are only just beginning to glimpse the limitless potential of the human mind.

CHECK LIST OF POINTS OR DISCUSSION TOPICS FROM VIDEOTAPES

I. _The Man With No Time For Beauty_

   A. Woodrow, surrounded by his personal culture--souvenirs and photographs out of his own past. Isn't that all right? Is he obliged to do more?

   B. Is this a distorted view of the retirement syndrome in the life of the average American?

   C. The child Woodrow is perhaps not typical of all children, even though the course uses children as symbols of the creative and open-minded approach to life that characterizes the humanist.

      1. Question: What can be done to encourage children to be imaginative and creative?

2. The child Woodrow obviously never saw television. Is this a plus factor?

D. Is it better to be naturally hostile toward the past, as Woodrow is, or to pretend to like it, as so many tourists do?

E. What makes The Last Supper perhaps the most famous painting in the world?

1. Its reputation for being the most famous painting in the world?

2. The fact that it is badly faded?

3. The fact that it was painted by a genius?

4. Is Leonardo a genius because of the painting?

F. The Mona Lisa and the principle of ambiguity in art.

1. Is the painting great despite the ambiguity of the face, or because of it?

2. Did Leonardo have a good press agent?

3. How do we know what Mona Lisa Giaconda really looked like? So how do we know it's a great painting?

G. The final shot--Woodrow at the fishing pier. Is he seeing the morning, or not?

II. The Way Of The Humanist

A. The importance of keeping the child alive within each of us.

Question: How can you gain experience as an adult without sacrificing the child's innocence?

B. Provide class with copies of the Keats sonnet.

1. Why would this poem appeal to the little girl when very little else in school excited her?

2. Is there any relationship between the poem and the circus?

3. Why is "a poet's death" the climatically beautiful thought that occurs to Keats?

4. How does this sonnet serve as a kind of overture for the whole course?

C. The humanist as mime.

1. Makeup turns the mime into a universal person, not narrowly involved in projecting only personal thoughts and feelings.

2. Like mimes, humanists sometimes have trouble being heard.

3. The two mimes stay more or less on the fringes of what happens; they exemplify the art of critical detachment.

D. The Walter Pater excerpt quoted as the mime lies dying can be found on page 529 of the text.

TEACHING ALTERNATIVES

The course as designed invites a show-then-talk format. If the videotape is especially provocative and/or if the class is a lively one, containing a lot of people who love to talk, the instructor will experience little difficulty keeping the course moving. Pace is very important, especially when so much time is devoted to watching television. Many students who have been overexposed to television, both in the home and in school, tend to fall into an immediate lethargy that even a provocative program may not be able to budge. Hence, it may be desirable, at least sometimes, to change the format. Alternatives are suggested for each module. It is, of course, assumed that no instructor would want to use them all.

Text (Chapters One and Two)

1. Divide the class into the "living" group and the "just existing" group, and ask each one to come up with a set of characteristics to share with the entire community.

2. Divide the class into two groups, one to be called the "New Brainers" and the other to be called the "Old Brainers." The latter is charged with preparing a comprehensive list of concerns from the reptilian and mammalian past, while the former is asked to do the same for the more recent history of the top brain.

3. At the conclusion of the first class period, take ten minutes and have each person show how much he or she has noticed already.

    What will the course be about?
    What is the instructor's name?
    What is the text title?
    How many tests will there be?
    How will the grades be determined?

The Man With No Time For Beauty

1. Invite those who have been abroad to suggest an itinerary to those who have never been out of the country, pointing out the esthetic high points. (There's always someone who has been to the same places, and who will object to the selection of high points.)

2. Divide the class into small groups. Each is to suppose itself a travel agency, and each is charged with the task of "selling" the local area to foreign tourists. What should be seen? And why? What is there in the area that will make the trip unforgettable?

The Way Of The Humanist

1. Invite class members singly or in pairs to pantomime both humanistic and non-humanistic actions, and have the class see whether communication has taken place.

2. Give each person 15 minutes to make a drawing of his or her "way" up to this point, suggesting symbolically each milestone choice that has been made. The final symbol should show the viewer where the person is now with respect to humanism.

JOURNAL TOPICS

Some instructors may offer the Journal as an alternate to particular examination, or indeed to all of them. Others may require a satisfactory score in the examinations, <u>plus</u> a minimum number of Journal entries in order for a student to qualify for an "A" in the course. For the external student, taking the series as a telecourse, the Journal can be a link with the campus, provided a faculty member or qualified assistant is there to read it and make comments.

One difficulty with Journals, however, is the invitation the student may suppose is there to rant on and on about nothing in particular, or not to take the time to think ideas through before committing them to paper. For each module, then, the instructor will find not only suggested Journal topics, but some guidelines students can be asked to follow.

A general rule of thumb is to assume that at least 30 minutes should be spent on each topic. This will help determine how many topics for each module would be suitable or acceptable. (Even a comment like "This doesn't seem like 30 minutes' worth" is seldom challenged.)

1. Define "human being" biologically, sociologically, culturally, ethnically, and humanistically.

2. List what you consider to be the major survival skills people need to have. Indicate why you think these are or are not enough to make life worthwhile.

3. Project your own version of a future society. Is it lacking in the humanities? If it isn't, how did they get there? If it is, does it matter to you?

4. Describe the humanistic resources of your area. Which ones do you avail yourself of? Which ones have you never patronized? Do you think it's worth going on to more of them than you now do?

5. Describe how you like to spend your leisure time. Do you see yourself as a humanist? Or is there some other label which fits better?

MODULAR INTERIOR STRUCTURE

If both videotapes are shown, the instructor can point out that one, *The Man with No Time for Beauty*, depicts a life without humanism, and the other, *The Way of the Humanist*, shows of course the opposite. The two programs are widely divergent in style, but they do have some links. In both there is a child and a reaction to a death. How does humanism affect both of these elements?

ESSAY QUESTIONS

The pilot test indicated that students do much better in the course when they are allowed to present their own views as well as to domonstrate cognitive retention. Essay questions can and probably should be included in each of the major examinations, but one or two can be given at the beginning or end of a class period, mainly as positive reinforcement to the students who are thinking, and as inducements to those who aren't.

I. Text

1. Have you known anyone like Woodrow Tatlock? If he were on trial for violating the spirit of the humanities, could you defend him? Could you press charges?

2. Does the first chapter view the humanities as accepting or resisting the fast pace of contemporary living? Explain.

3. Summing up what Chapter Two has to say about the human mind, would you say that humanity is at the peak of its powers, past its peak, or still in its infancy?

II. The Man With No Time For Beauty

1. Suggest two ways in which Woodrow Tatlock could improve the quality of his life.

2. What were Woodrow's motives in signing up for the European tour? In your opinion, why and when should one take such a trip?

3. Not everyone can afford to take a trip to Europe. Is such a thing necessary for a complete life?

4. The film suggests that sitting at a sidewalk cafe and watching people walk by is a valid esthetic activity. Do you agree?

5. Describe one leisure-time activity Europeans appear to enjoy that is not characteristic of Americans.

III. The Way Of The Humanist

1. Why is the circus a better metaphor for humanism than the little girl's schoolroom?

2. Why is poetry the little girl's favorite subject?

3. How would you define sensitivity as a quality possessed by both mimes?

4. Why does the film end with the main character as a little girl again?

5. What is the significance of the fact that the little girl is holding the mime's hat and cane at the end of the film?

MODULE II

ART AND THE ARTIST

TEACHING OVERVIEW

Some instructors who have taught the program since the pilot test reported that they had omitted both Modules II and III. One said it was in the interest of time; another, that he did not feel comfortable teaching either art or music. True, both modules are, on the surface, somewhat more specialized, less clearly interdisciplinary than the others, and the temptation may be there for people whose background is drama or philosophy, for example, to bypass these units. The advice is to give them a try. The approach is consistent with that taken in the rest of the course. Art and music are self-discovery disciplines. They are components of the humanist's life. They are not presented technically or historically.

Instead of history, the text chapter is presented as the peg on which to hang the lecture or discussion of the Aristotelian idea of _imitation_. The artist is shown as an imitator, sometimes of reality as it is, sometimes of nature's own creative process. Art can seek to reproduce the appearance of things, or it can seek to alter existing reality by bringing something new into the world. The important thing is to come to each artist with an open mind, not a preconceived opinion of what art should be or do.

The artist's need to bring something new into existence is analyzed in the first video program, Art: Tell Me What I Am, which adds the same metaphor we found in the first module--the artist is the child within us, reaching out to alter the environment.

The second video program, Divine Discontent, seeks to demystify artists by showing them to be human and, therefore, vulnerable like the rest of us. Their art is the happy result of a distinctly unhappy state of tension between them and the world around them. This program is an example of how this course attempts to establish a human relationship between the titans and the student.

CHECK LIST OF POINTS OR DISCUSSION TOPICS FROM TEXT

1. The four quotations which introduce the chapter give us a broad range of insights into the artist's psychology. (Students are especially fond of "getting into" Robert Thiele's laconic definition.)

2. The best point of departure is mimesis, Aristotle's marvelous word, which we translate loosely as "imitation." Point out how our culture has devalued this term, and how it now almost always means false. But true imitation is behind every artistic venture. Its viable meaning is "recreating the process of nature." The artist brings new things into existence. Sometimes they look like other things in nature; sometimes they resemble only themselves.

3. The newly discovered cave paintings at Lascaux may shed new light on early artists, and their level of sophistication. Originally believed to be a primitive means of making quarry more plentiful, cave paintings may be examples of the urge

to create, to imitate. Most of the animals depicted at Lascaux could not have roamed in the vicinity.

4. Betty Edwards's right-brain approach to drawing has had much (documented) success with beginning art students. Those enrolled in THE ART OF BEING HUMAN may need more detailed explanation of what makes these drawing exercises <u>right</u>-brain rather than <u>left</u>-brain involvements.

5. The students can turn to the text centerfold and look at the color reproduction of Goya's <u>Saturn Devouring His Son</u> during a discussion of whether such an unpleasant subject can result in a beautiful work of art. Does the artist have the right to do anything he or she wishes?

6. Why does marble not want to look soft? Why is art "pretending there is no artist"?

7. How did the invention of photography influence artists in the nineteenth century?

8. The section titled "The Artist and Society" has a central (if tentative) thesis--in less secure cultures artists are strongly nurtured, and tend to become spokespeople for their people; in more secure cultures artists can become alienated, often cynical.

9. Students generally love to discuss the matter of artist versus billpayer. During the 1960's sentiment usually was on the side of the unconventional artist, who did "his thing." Nowadays, perhaps more can be said for the billpayer.

10. Since "Guernica" is right there in the chapter (page 92), why not devote a little time to a close study of the work, asking the students especially whether a more direct (realistic) statement would have been more--or less--powerful?

CHECK LIST OF POINTS OR DISCUSSION TOPICS FROM VIDEOTAPES

I. <u>Art, Tell Me What I Am</u>
<u>Art, Tell Us Who We Are</u>

A. The narrator assumes he is an artist, and semi-apologizes for his burning need to project himself onto the wall. How does someone know he is an artist? Or is the need proof enough?

B. Art tells us who we are, and is often the only testimony to the nature of an entire culture (e.g., the Mayan civilization). Why does it matter that some record be left behind?

C. Colors are what emotions look like.

1. Why are orange and yellow "up" colors, full of hope and vitality?

2. Why are black and grey linked to depression and death?

3. What are the colors of:

spirituality	grief
feelings of unworth	passion
paranoia	hunger
treachery	contentment
life-affirmation	anger

D. Juxtaposition in art of unconnected or dissonant things.

E. Lines in art: horizontal, vertical, diagonal, curving. Why do these types of lines have dramatically different effects?

F. If all you knew about modern art was what the artists in the film have to say, how would you summarize what was going on in art at the moment?

II. <u>Divine Discontent</u>

A. The program title. "Discontent" does not mean what it usually does.

B. Why are geniuses often out of alignment with the rest of society?

C. Some geniuses have become so arrogant in their isolation that they openly flaunt their sense of irresponsibility toward others. Do they have the right?

D. The implication is that Michelangelo was never really satisfied with anything he did. Does genius have rewards? What kind?

E. "Terribilitá" as the transcendent quality in Michelangelo.

F. Goya - Art as the gateway to the unconscious.

Question: Why do I need to involve myself in another person's anguish?

G. One cannot imagine Van Gogh's painting in the style he developed if his life had been serene and happy.

Question: Is greatness after one's death a good trade-off?

TEACHING ALTERNATIVES

<u>Text</u>

1. This exercise can be used to give each person extra credit.

Instructions: Find a quiet corner. Use a large blank piece of paper and a Flair pen or magic marker. (Announce in advance that this paraphernalia is to be brought to class.)

Task: Imagine that you are no longer here. You are, of course, remembered in the thoughts and conversation of others, and there are your letters and other reminders of you. On the paper in front of you create a silent witness to your having existed, one you believe will be the <u>real</u> you.

2. Another extra credit exercise.

Instructions: Find a quiet corner. Use a heavy piece of poster paper and some marking implement(s) of your choice (such as a paint brush, a Flair pen, a magic marker, a set of crayons, etc.)

Task: Pick any abstract subject (religion, world hunger, the energy crisis, grounds for hope, etc.) and make a statement about it through some two-dimensional figure or design.

Afterwards: Hold an art exhibit in which the artists share their statements with each other.

3. Quick ten-minute beginning-of-class exercise.

   Task: On any sheet of paper do a diagram of this classroom and either draw or in some way indicate how you would redesign it to create a more esthetic environment.

   The sharing will use up the rest of the class time--and then some.

4. Announce that each person is to bring a bar of soap (bath size) to class the following session, along with a small knife for cutting.

   Task: Do a soap sculpture that represents this class.

   Some people will naturally do better sculptures than others. Ask the sculptors (supposedly at random) to describe their intention and, in their opinion, degree of success. This can lead into a meaningful discussion of the phrase "resistance of the medium."

<u>Art, Tell Me What I Am</u>

1. Divide the class into small groups. Give each one around 15 minutes to design a kinetic sculpture, using every member of the group. The sculpture should embody a definite subject, or make a definite statement, which the other members of the class must be able to interpret.

   Afterwards: Have the entire class vote on the single most original and "artistic" sculpture.

2. The graphic graffiti wall makes for an exciting class. Butcher's wrapping paper is all that's needed. Tack it up around the room. Give each person a magic marker, and then say "Go to it."

   To maintain some degree of control, one may wish to stipulate a theme or some basic task, such as: express righteous anger in symbolic form; make a blatant statement in disguise (non-verbal); tell us what's wrong with the school (non-verbal).

<u>Divine Discontent</u>

One of the tragic ironies in the history of the humanities is the inability of many great people to find recognition during their lifetime. Van Gogh is surely a prime example.

Discuss this point briefly, then divide the class into small groups, each one charged with a particular area of concern (e.g., films, theater, television, art, sculpture, education, etc.) The group is to discuss people who are doing very important, perhaps great, things in that area but who are not enjoying widespread recognition and acceptance. One such person is to be finally singled out, and then a spokesperson for the group will pay homage to that person before the rest of the class.

JOURNAL TOPICS

1. Like the young Woodrow in the program "The Man with No Time for Beauty," children tend to be highly imitative in the Aristotelian sense of the word. That program goes on to show how adults like Woodrow become progressively less imitative. How can the world of the artist be used by each of us as a guarantee that we won't become Woodrows?

2. Art is often produced from the dynamic tension which develops between an artist's drive, and the resistance of the medium. But why limit the good things of this world to art? How can one use different kinds of resistance to good effect in ordinary life? Example: Are there any benefits to living in a household governed by very tight rules, which restrict one's choice of activities?

3. What reasons can you think of for justifying the fact that an enormous curtain, stretched between two mountains, is called art by its "creator," and recognized as art by some critics?

4. One intellectual historian singled out Picasso as one of the mightiest persons who ever lived, in terms of the amount of change he was directly responsible for. Describe the changes made by Picasso, not necessarily limited to the art world as such.

5. If our society were to vanish like that of the Mayas, described in Art, Tell Me What I Am, leaving behind only art and artifacts, single out some specific things (art works, buildings, utensils, important items, etc.) which would constitute the best summing up of what we were like.

6. Cheese should not be green, and beautiful ladies should not have ugly, protruding teeth. Artists used to idealize and perfect the

world as it is. Now it seems that some artists deliberately distort things. Why do they do it? Why is it art?

7. A number of years ago the philosopher Peter Bertocci coined the happy phrase "creative insecurity," by which he meant all the wonderful, imaginative things people do to compensate for or transcend personal conflicts and crises. His idea was that people should be very grateful for all the obstacles life continually throws in their path, for without these, they would never have the chance to find out how truly ingenious and resourceful they really are. If you had the choice, would you like your whole life to be totally fulfilled, or would you prefer a measure of creative insecurity? Be specific.

8. Would you rather be a relatively stable, modestly successful, but essentially obscure person all your life, or a genius like Van Gogh even if the price were a lack of recognition, and eventually madness?

MODULAR INTERIOR STRUCTURE

The two TV films have a definite relationship. The first (*Art, Tell Me What I Am*) somewhat fancifully describes the creative process itself--what goes on inside the mind of an artist. The second (*Divine Discontent*) shows the awful price that is sometimes paid by those in whom this process operates in over-abundance. In its starkest form, the interior structure points out "*This is what it is*," and then asks, "*Is it worth the struggle*?"

The intent is to humanize the process--to bring the mind of an artist within striking distance of the average student. Even to come away with the feeling that the struggle was not worth the price is to have been more humanly involved with art than is frequently the case.

The overall purpose of the module is not necessarily to "sell" art to the students, but to intensity their appreciation for artists as human beings struggling to express themselves. Without empathy for the artist there can be no lasting concern for art.

ESSAY QUESTIONS

I. Text

1. One modern artist sat inside an air-conditioning vent, audibly taking pleasure in sex fantasies while people in the gallery looked at his work. He claimed the sounds from the vent were crucial factors in his art. Is there a limit to what can be art?

2. Does the fact that a piece of sculpture looks exactly like a giant ice bag detract from its being art? Why an ice bag?

3. Time was when national academies composed of great critics and scholars had the power to decide what did or did not constitute art. Was that a good idea?

4. In communist societies the state still has control over the arts. Should art be answerable to the state? To anybody?

5. If you were or are an artist, would you be or are you alienated within the dominant modes of our society? Explain.

6. Using an appropriate artist as an illustration, explain the phrase "resistance of the medium."

II. Art, Tell Me What I Am

1. The narrator's painting of the wall is an example of street art. Suggest at least two other ways in which people could have an artistic rather than random environment.

2. One of the interviewed artists called a six-foot block of wood a self-portrait because he was six feet tall. Suppose you had to do such a portrait of yourself. What material would you use, and what would the final product look like?

3. If you were to vanish tomorrow, what one silent witness could tell people who and what you were?

III. Divine Discontent

1. What does the title mean? Give one example of your own divine discontents.

2. Of the four geniuses considered in the film Divine Discontent, which one in your opinion derived the least from his genius?

3. We generally think of David as being small in comparison with Goliath. Yet Michelangelo made David into an enormous statue. Why?

4. Using specific examples, explain the term "terribilitá" as a way of describing Michelangelo's work.

5. Goya came to Madrid from the country in order to please the court and win favor. What made him decide to paint in his own style, no matter who liked his work or did not?

6. Unamuno, the philosopher, said to the artist: "May God deny you peace, but give you glory." If you had to choose, which would it be? Why?

SURVEY 1 PRESCRIPTIONS

At the conclusion of the second, fourth, sixth, eighth, tenth, twelfth, fourteenth, and fifteenth modules in the study guide, the student will find a survey containing at least 20 multiple-choice questions covering the material just studied. These questions can be prototypes of what the student can expect in the way of objective testing, or they can be helpful in focusing the material in the course. Some questions ask for straight cognitive recall; others are clearly affective in nature, asking for the "best possible" response or, in a few instances, an extremely personal response which is neither right nor wrong.

For instructors, these surveys should demonstrate how objective measurements can be used without sacrificing the chance to see how much critical discernment the student is developing. A number of items call for interpretation; a number, for synthesis; a number, for application, and so on. Combined with short answer essay topics, the survey-type questions should provide a highly adequate evaluation system for the course.

With very large classes--and where the technology is available--computers can be programmed to grade <u>and</u> to respond to these surveys. For this reason, suggested responses (or prescriptions) are provided in this manual. The instructor may want to use these prescriptions to give the student more than the correct answer, especially since some of the survey items do not lend themselves to a right/wrong dichotomy. (<u>NOTE</u>: In the survey prescriptions, under the <u>Answers</u> column, n/a indicates that there is no "right" answer. Each response receives a prescription.)

SURVEY 1 PRESCRIPTIONS

<u>Answers</u>

1 1. Those who responded #2, 3, 4, or 5 receive the prescription:

In the film, <u>Art: Tell Me What I Am/Art: Tell Us Who We Are</u>, the narrator tells us that while vertical lines express stability and order, diagonals express motion and urgency. Examples would be Goya's paintings, "The Third of May" and "Saturn Devouring His Son."

4 2. Those who responded #1, 2, 3, or 5 receive the prescription:

(See note on p. 71)
Empathy is ordinarily defined as the ability to put oneself in another's place. A basic example occurs when you watch a tightrope walker at the circus and find yourself swaying from side to side, as if you were up there. Empathy in literature occurs when you project yourself into the character and feel everything he or she is experiencing. In real life, empathy is the ability to see beyond oneself, to see things from the perspective of others.

1 3. Those who responded #2, 3, 4, or 5 receive the prescription:

Please note that, according to the wording or the question, all options except one are correct. Humanists do indeed believe that people do not live for the government or their jobs, that living is a learned art, that humanity need serve no purpose but its own, and that in order to fulfill themselves, people must be free to choose between significant alternatives. If it is true that people must choose their own destinies, then it cannot also be true that people are born with a natural talent for making the most of their lives.

5 4. Those who responded #1, 2, 3, or 4 receive the prescription:

The little girl prefers to look through the window and let her imagination carry her to far-off places. It is only when the subject in class is poetry that her imagination is stimulated. Perhaps there is nothing wrong with imagination. Too often this is the first human attribute we are willing to sacrifice in the interest of "practical" matters.

Answers

1 5. Those who responded #2, 3, 4, or 5 receive the prescription:

Showing a strong loyalty to time-proven beliefs might at first glance seem to be a characteristic of an effective human life. The word "loyalty" is usually associated with the upright, decent person; but there is a difference between blind, unyielding loyalty and that loyalty which is willing to reexamine itself frequently. There are few causes or beliefs which will not bear such reexamination, and humanists must never allow an allegiance to tradition to close their minds.

n/a 6. Each response receives a prescription:

(1) Look around; you may be pleasantly surprised.

(2) Why are you unconcerned? If you don't try something, you will never know how much it may benefit you.

(3) Many offer this excuse, but frequently "I don't have time" really means "I'm basically not interested." You have to experience something before you decide it has nothing to offer you. Chances are you won't decide that at all.

(4) Good for you. I hope this course will offer you a chance to report on some of the recent experiences you have had.

(5) I hope that by the end of the course you will have decided which ones you want to explore. Perhaps you will already have expanded your range.

4 7. Those who responded #1, 2, 3, or 5 receive the prescription:

(1) If Woodrow believed the painting did not deserve its fame, he would not have been so troubled by his inability to appreciate it.

(2) Woodrow's remarks to himself while driving his truck to the fishing pier do not indicate that he knows why people revere the painting.

(3) True, Woodrow does try the "one eye" trick but, even after he has done so and heard the lady's lecture on the painting, he cannot share her enthusiasm. For one thing, he cannot agree that all faces are mysterious and beautiful. He does not believe his face has beauty.

(5) Woodrow indicates at the beginning of the film that most people admire art because it is expensive. He may still feel this way about the "Mona Lisa," but there is no indication from what he says that this is his final attitude.

2 8. Those who responded #1, 3, 4, or 5 receive the prescription:

Nelson Rockefeller, grandson of John D., had a famous bout with the Mexican muralist Diego Rivera when, during the 1930's, he commissioned the latter to provide a colorful and decorative wall piece for the lobby of Rockefeller Center on Fifth Avenue, New York. Rivera placed a gigantic head of Lenin in the center of his mural, a fact which made Rockefeller distinctly unhappy. Pope Julius II commissioned Michelangelo to do four sculptures in marble for his own tomb, did not like what the artist came up with, and cancelled the order. These famous incidents raise the perennial question: Who should call the turn?

4 9. Those who responded #1, 2, 3, or 5 receive the prescription:

Since intensity and brilliance are omnipresent characteristics in Van Gogh's work, the only appropriate comparison (among the options provided) is with the dynamic quality in Michelangelo's sculptures. Chiaroscuro is not a technique particularly associated with Michelangelo, nor is distortion a characteristic of his most noble achievements. There is no evidence that Michelangelo preferred flawed to perfect marble, though it is supposedly true that the artist was able to buy cheaply the giant block from which he fashioned the David because of a flaw in the marble. But the statue is great despite the flaw, not because of it.

3 10. Each incorrect response receives a prescription:

(1) This option is indeed a possibility, except that it does not say quite enough about an artist's motives. The correct answer, which is that the narrator needed to put himself in the external world, states a relationship between the artist and the wall; "Because it's there" does not.

(2) Let us hope this would not be the artist's or anybody else's motive for doing something unless they are victims of an extremely corrupt government. Our

artist in the film tells you in so many words that he wants to see himself "out there" in the places around him.

(4) By definition, a vandal is a destroyer, not a creator, so we surely would not consider such a person an artist. Our artist in the film tells you in so many words that he needs to see himself out there in the external world.

(5) Artists who are interested in political propaganda do not want to hide it behind brush strokes. They want to use their talent to make their bold statement. Besides, our artist in the film tells you in so many words that he needs to see himself out there in the external world.

3 11. Those who responded #1, 2, 4, or 5 receive the prescription:

In matters of interpretation, an absolute right/wrong polarity is difficult to achieve. We can only hope to come as close as possible to the best possible assessment of the meaning. The phrase "divine discontent" is especially subtle, for it refers not to literal dissatisfaction, but to a certain kind of frustration that has enormous creative consequences. Options 1, 2, and 4 all deal with dissatisfaction, while Option 5 appears to have nothing to do with discontent--divine or otherwise. But Michelangelo's burning desire to create a work worthy of God is indeed an example of a gigantic frustration that drove the artist to mammoth achievements which merit the adjective "divine."

4 12. Those who responded #1, 2, 3, or 5 receive the prescription:

In Aristotelian terminology, imitating does not mean literally reproducing the appearance of things but, rather, trying to recreate the soul of things. The imitation of human grief in a Greek tragedy does not show us how people in real life actually grieve, but what grieving means. So we can say that the imitative artist is one who creates, just as nature creates.

4 13. Those who responded #1, 2, 3, or 5 receive the prescription:

People like Woodrow Tatlock dislike change, and limit their experiences to what is familiar--what reflects

Answers

their own long-held tastes and convictions. The result is stagnation--simply waiting for the end--rather than using new experiences to recreate oneself in more fully human ways.

5 14. Those who responded #1, 2, 3, or 4 receive the prescription:

In his pursuit of material goals, Woodrow Tatlock has been too busy for "the finer things in life." As a result, he has settled for too little--a life far less human than that of Woodrow the child.

1 15. Those who responded #2, 3, 4, or 5 receive the prescription:

The technique of chiaroscuro (a sharp contrast between brilliant light and deep shadow) immediately identifies Rembrandt's paintings. An example is "Night Watch."

5 16. Those who responded #1, 2, 3, or 4 receive the prescription:

A number of times throughout the film, "The Man With No Time for Beauty," we are shown a flashback of Woodrow Tatlock as a child. In each instance the child is excited over a new experience--a bird, a merry-go-round, the morning. In contrast, the adult Woodrow is shown rejecting new experiences. Hence, the answer is: An openness to life.

5 17. Those who responded #1, 2, 3, or 4 receive the prescription:

This question calls for an interpretation. We have here an example of a symbol that does not invite one interpretation to the exclusion of other possibilities. Surely, the mime's humanism sees nothing wrong with escaping from drab reality, provided one does not escape permanently. Nor is there any essential conflict among the intuitive, rational, idealistic approaches to life. All are part of the humanist's way. The hat and cane, which represent the humanist's essence, no doubt suggest many more interpretations.

4 18. Those who responded #1, 2, 3, or 5 receive the prescription:

The first notable use of perspective (the art of making

figures appear three dimensional on a plane or curved surface) is attributed to Giotto Di Bondone (C. 1276-C. 1337), who belongs to the very early Italian Renaissance. Some art historians, however, maintain that Giotto did not produce a completely authentic perspective. Rather, he introduced the principle of placing figures in different vertical positions on the canvas in order to suggest accurate spatial relationships. The illusion of depth is not profound in Giotto, it is true, but the artist can certainly be given credit as a pioneer. Soon after, the art of perspective began to flower.

3 19. Those who responded #1, 2, 4, or 5 receive the prescription:

Photography came into being in 1839 with Louis Daguerre's creation of a process by which images could be fixed on metal plates. Within a few decades photography had proved it could capture reality better than painters. Many artists agreed, especially those who came to be known as impressionists. They abandoned the imitation of reality in favor of rendering subjective experience on canvas.

4 20. Those who responded #1, 2, 3, or 5 receive the prescription:

Picasso's "Guernica" is an example of cubism, a technique of painting in which people and objects are not represented realistically, but rather they are rendered as geometric forms. In "Guernica," jagged lines and sharp angles convey a sense of pain and dread.

3 21. Those who responded #1, 2, 4, or 5 receive the prescription:

While we have no way of knowing how much cynicism may have been experienced inwardly by the other artist cited in this question, Francisco Goya is the only one whose works betray the emotion. Particularly in his later paintings, Goya seems obsessed with the dark and ugly side of human nature.

2 22. Those who responded #1, 3, 4, or 5 receive the prescription:

Answers

Sigmund Freud, of course, wasn't an artist at all. While Goya, Van Gogh, and Oldenburg are giants of art, their work tends uniformly to proclaim their unique styles. But Picasso seems never to have been satisfied with one style--his work exhibits a phenomenal range, from realism to cubism, from the most representational recreation of figures to the radical alteration of reality into geometric design.

2 23. Those who responded #1, 3, 4, or 5 receive the prescription:

Impressionism was a major 19th century movement in art which rebelled against rules and established a new, subjective manner of painting. Idealism is not a label given to an art movement, while paintings we can call "romantic" tend to revive older styles. Realism does not express subjective states of mind, and chiaroscuro is the technique of contrasting light and shadow in a painting.

4 24. Those who responded #1, 2, 3, or 5 receive the prescription:

Stone and canvas resist the artist in the sense that the medium through which the artist works never immediately suggests the uses to which it can be put. Most of us would just look at a piece of marble or a blank canvas without knowing what to do with it. Thus, the medium defies us to transform it, but the great artists are equal to the challenge.

3 25. Those who responded #1, 2, 4, or 5 receive the prescription:

In the program "Divine Discontent," the narrator explains that Michelangelo was angry at first when Pope Julius ordered him to paint the frescoes in the Sistine Chapel, for Michelangelo considered himself a sculptor, not a painter. It was a conflict between the artist's right to define himself and his medium, and the employer's right to dictate terms.

Answers

3 26. Those who responded #1, 2, 4, or 5 receive the prescription:

We would know virtually nothing of Mayan culture were it not for the sculpture and architectural monuments which survived after the civilization itself had disappeared.

2 27. Those who responded #1, 3, 4, or 5 receive the prescription:

The statement is made about Vincent Van Gogh. These qualities are evident in "Starry Night."

2 28. Those who responded #1, 3, 4, or 5 receive the prescription:

Goya's later work raises the question of whether a work of art can be pleasant to look at if it is to give esthetic satisfaction. Neither the subject matter nor the appearance of paintings like "The Third of May" and "Saturn Devouring His Son" (see color plates in text) is likely to produce agreeable sensations in the viewer. Rather, by shocking the viewer's sensibilities, these paintings communicate terror, cruelty, and the painter's cynicism. Earlier theories of art would not have considered such emotions as proper responses. Goya was one of the first artists whose work raised the question of whether any strong emotional response to art is valid. The issue is still far from decided, but it could be said that much modern art would have to be disclaimed if one insisted on only tranquil responses.

NOTE: Item #2 in Study Guide Survey 1 should be:

Woodrow Tatlock, so goes the text, was most lacking in empathy. The best meaning of empathy would be which of the following?

1. being charitable toward others
2. enjoying a peak experience
3. the ability to alienate oneself when necessary
4. the ability to see beyond oneself
5. the ability to relate significant events to one's own life.

MODULE III

MUSIC: THE PLANNED ENVIRONMENT

TEACHING OVERVIEW

Anyone who has ever taught a music unit in a humanities survey course knows that nothing tends to deaden a class as effectively as long periods of listening to records, or watching musicians perform on film. True, here and there one will spot an excited or blissful face; this or that piece does indeed strike a responsive chord in this or that listener. But on the whole, it is difficult to make students "like" music by making them sit there and take huge amounts of it at one time.

The text takes an oblique approach. Defining music as the shaped sounds between silences, it has as much to say about silence as about music. For the instructor who feels extremely uncomfortable within a module that seems to call for a specialist, an underlying theme of silence, what it means, and why some tend to avoid it, can work. The chapter contains some psychology and social science as well as a general introduction to musical elements. There is reference to Future Shock and the addiction to noise which characterizes our culture. There are statements about rock 'n roll, folk songs and what they connote, as well as commentary on the achievement of Beethoven in music, and of jazz as art and as social expression. There is an invitation to experience the unfamiliar sounds of contemporary music so that one can grow in both artistic taste and in self-knowledge.

Both TV programs below should be enough to handle the performance element which has to be involved in a unit on music, but even these have been designed to teach points rather than to substitute for live concert experiences. The second film, Jazz/Bach, which features very prominent musicians, has less talk and more music--and the longest segment of pure music contains a specially arranged jazz piece based on Bach themes, and generally wins favor with the students. The first film, Sound To Music, parallels the psychological comments in the text and, while students will enjoy the playing of Cassandria Hanna and Alfred Pinkston, there are a number of cognitive points to discuss when the TV set is turned off. Instructors need not feel "abandoned" and at the mercy of whatever discussion the old stand-by, "How did the music make you feel?", generates.

CHECK LIST OF POINTS OR DISCUSSION TOPICS FROM TEXT

1. We exist within two kinds of audio environments: one is unplanned, random, and sometimes maddening--especially for those who inhabit densely populated cities; the other is planned, and under control of people--music, by us and for us.

2. Music as the shaped sounds between silences. One must learn to appreciate silence before one can appreciate music. (Note: Playing the "Funeral March" from Beethoven's Eroica lends special reinforcement to this point.)

3. The main musical elements:

    <u>intervals</u> - variance in pitch between tones

    <u>pitch</u> - low or high sounds produced by speed of sound vibrations

    <u>rhythm</u> - (Webster) regular recurrence of grouped strong and weak beats, or heavily and lightly accented tones

    <u>melody</u> - significant arrangement of tones in a flowing sequence; or, as in Romantic music, a highly individualized arrangement, meant to be sensuous and appealing, and differentiated from what precedes and follows

    <u>timbre</u> - the characteristic sound of each music-producing agent, including the human voice

    <u>harmony</u> - two or more tones sung or sounded simultaneously and producing an esthetic effect

4. Music as the external anchor of the feelings; music as what emotion sounds like. The important point to make here is that helping us identify ourselves emotionally is only one of the things music can do. It is not necessary that <u>all</u> music be rooted in and be aimed at the emotions.

5. Bach:

    a. epitomized Baroque style (complexity and improvisation)
    b. work illustrates the magnificent tension between restriction of form and composer's need for liberation

6. Folk music - helps groups achieve identity and cohesiveness

7. Spirituals - make possible the release of profound sadness, as well as religious ecstasy

8. Gospel - notable example of liberation achieved through an underlying rhythmic and melodic control

9. Country-and-Western tradition - survival of the Anglo-Irish sorrowful ballad

10. Beethoven - the forms he had "shrank"; the feelings of the man expanded, found release through the enlargement of the forms; but the forms are as controlled as they are enormous--allowing the feelings to surround but never engulf us.

CHECK LIST OF POINTS OR DISCUSSION TOPICS FROM VIDEOTAPES

I. Sound To Music

A. Briefly, the title. The relationship between random sounds and music.

1. This could be a good point at which to introduce the principle of avant-garde music, which is modestly sampled in the film.

2. If time permits, one could play a few bars of John Cage. Question: When do random sounds become music even if they still seem like random sounds?

B. Narrator maintains that loud rock music makes us passive and non-reflective, that it deadens the sensibilities. Agree?

C. Plainsong - Why is its simple flowing line spiritual?

Significance of unison singing in plainsong.

D. Harmony - The principle of sounding or singing more than one note at the same time.

Sometimes harmony falls pleasantly on the ear; sometimes it is dissonance. Why we need both experiences.

E. Melody - A combination of notes that form a significant unity.

1. Versions produced by Romantic composers still set the standard for many people's concept of what melody is.

2. Aversion of many to unfamiliar combinations.

3. Importance of expanding one's toleration of unusual melodies.

F. How music sounds like a place or a period.

1. Why does New York music sound a certain way? What is the New York sound?

2. Is there a California sound? A Southern sound?

3. Why composers today may not sound like yesterday.

II. Jazz/Bach

A. Jazz/Bach defined as the ongoing musical tradition of humanity's rebellious spirit.

B. Jazz/Bach as a musical parallel to yin/yang. Bach as the formalism, jazz the negation of form that still depends upon form for its existence.

C. Bach himself, however, contains both yin and yang--the restraints of the form and the energy of liberation.

D. Jazz also contains formalism and improvisation. Hence the debt to Bach acknowledged by jazz musicians.

E. Ira Sullivan's contention that jazz is spiritual music. In his view, jazz improvisation is the effort of the musician's soul to achieve union with God.

TEACHING ALTERNATIVES

Text

1. It can be a mind-boggling experience for the student to come to the first class in a music unit and, instead of having someone turn on a stereo or punch a "play" button on a videocassette deck, be told to sit there in the seat, eyes shut, and be absolutely quiet. Ten minutes of complete silence can introduce this module most effectively.

   Following the soundless prelude, one can hold an open discussion of the difference between real silence and our noisy environments, or one can show the first videotape Sound To Music with good effect.

2. If each of us had no music inside, no one could have invented music. At all events, each possesses the fundamental need for song. So why not allow the need to express and fulfill itself?

   Ask every class member to compose a song of at least a minute's duration, and be prepared to perform it for the others.

3. Nothing lifts a class quite so high as to sit in a circle and wait until someone starts to sing. It is almost always a

familiar group-enhancing piece, and the others will automatically join in. Whether it's "I've Been Workin' On the Railroad" or "Frere Jacques" or "Old MacDonald," the power of song is instantly demonstrated.

Sound To Music

Show the film, and then divide the class into groups. Charge each group with working out a strategy whereby they might introduce an absolutely hostile group of students to the glories of music. The report to the rest of the class can be brief or quite elaborate, involving the use of records and tapes, etc.

One can produce a highly effective class, no matter what the subject matter, by having the students create an imaginary adversary and then finding a way to "win."

Jazz/Bach

The title of the film is a new word coined from existing words that had never before, to our knowledge, been juxtaposed. But sometimes we have to create unusual combinations in order to make a point.

Show the film, then divide into small groups. Each is to be charged with the task of making as long a list as possible of word coinages, using in every instance two terms like Jazz and Bach which, when placed side-by-side, constitute a way of shedding light on some aspect of human experience.

Afterwards, the group can share their coinages.

JOURNAL TOPICS

1. Go through the text and single out any two musical elements you can relate to your own personality and style of life.

2. Are you much given to solitude and silence? Or do you prefer to live amid sounds? If so, what kind of sounds? If you prefer silence, why? What does silence do for you?

3. People who never go out without carrying a transistor radio, and who play their car radios at high noise levels, must surely develop in a radically different manner from those who do not require continual sound stimulation. Suggest differences.

4. What are the latest trends in rock music? What are they saying about our culture?

5. Describe your own musical preferences. Do you tend to be one-sided? Have you a broad range of options? What do you learn about yourself from considering these preferences?

6. Which musical selection in either videotape did you like the most? What is the basis of your choice?

7. When most people think of "melody," they think of a Romantic piece by Tchaikowsky or Rachmaninoff. What does melody mean to you?

8. Consider the sociological background of jazz in its origins. Jazz is still with us. What is its statement nowadays?

9. What makes Beethoven no doubt the giant of music?

10. The 60's went in for a great deal of folk music. Is it still popular? If the answer is positive, why? If the answer is negative, what has taken its place?

MODULAR INTERIOR STRUCTURE

The two films offer a contrast between the general view of music presented in Sound To Music and the specific instances of musical genius presented in Jazz/Bach. If one wishes to connect the two (and this is by no means necessary), one can emphasize the examples of dynamic tension in the first program; e.g., the control exercised over passionate sorrow in the blues; the underlying rhythmic principles in the modern pieces, which keep them from formlessness. Then one can ask the students to view Jazz/Bach in terms of a detailed illustration of how a basic conflict between emotion and form creates music in different ages. This opens the door for an interesting discussion of the many rock stars and bands today whose musical rationale seems to be "throw all tension to the winds."

ESSAY QUESTIONS

I. Text

1. Why is it said that, in order to appreciate music, you have to be able to handle silence?

2. Pythagoras, whose first love was mathematics, was also a pioneer in the art of music. Is there a connection between the two?

3. In times of national crisis, music helps to mobilize the feelings of a people and helps to create unity. Do we have any crisis music today?

4. Americans are supposedly fonder of the bass than the treble, and fonder of brass and percussion than the string section. Suggest a reason.

II. Sound To Music

1. Which musical piece touched you the most? (If you can't remember the title or composer, describe the piece.) Why did it have an effect on you?

2. Does the film present rock music fairly, or unfairly? State why.

3. Why is plainsong considered spiritual and polyphony secular?

4. What is meant by the term "dynamics" relative to Beethoven's music?

5. Beethoven used a great deal of dissonance, which horrified some of his audiences at first. Why would a composer want to horrify his listeners?

6. What makes a person devote his or her life to a particular musical instrument?

III. Jazz/Bach

1. Would Bach have enjoyed being on the same bill with Duke Ellington and Charlie Parker?

2. Is jazz popular with young people today? Why, or why not?

3. If Bach and Charlie Parker do it, then improvising must be an important aspect of being human. How much improvising are you able to do? What holds you back?

4. Blacks are quite dominant in American musical tradition. Why do you think this is so?

5. What do Bach and Joplin have in common?

MODULE IV

PHILOSOPHY: MORAL VALUES

TEACHING OVERVIEW

The subject is vast, and the time is limited. The advice is to restrict oneself to a particular line of inquiry, and not attempt to deal with all of the material in class. The text chapter appears to pose no great difficulty for students, who can be held responsible for a good deal more than can be discussed. If instructors announce the discrepancy in advance, they are free to emphasize their own priorities in the matter of moral education.

There is, however, one common theme running through the text chapter and both videotapes: _The sanctions of moral behavior_. What value system or authoritative force justifies an action, or says that one course of action is right while another is wrong? One could easily build the unit on this pervasive issue. Students in the pilot test found it stimulating, and all instructors reported good class participation.

A possible procedure would be to divide the sanctions into meaningful groupings. For example:

religion
- word of God
- sacred documents
- traditions originating in religious teachings

rationalism

Socrates--moral knowledge, universal and unchanging

existentialists--in choosing for oneself, one chooses for all; The Anguish of Abraham--agony of choosing

situationalism

no universals

each question examined on own merits

the question of whose interpretation prevails

A decade ago the most popular issue in moral philosophy was the "do your thing" option. The interest is still there, though "do your thing" no longer seems to be the slogan. Rather, students are interested in discussing why, since everyone is motivated by self-interest, this and this alone should not be the determining factor in a moral system. "Self-interest" or some other appropriate label can be added to the group of sanctions. Or else, the instructor can introduce the subject, asking whether "self-interest" belongs in a list of sanctions.

One can spend a profitable week analyzing these questions. Are moral values based upon anything except self-interest even possible? Or can we even have a morality when values do not transcend self-interest?

CHECK LIST OF POINTS OR DISCUSSION TOPICS FROM TEXT

1. Working definition of a moral value: The basis of making a free choice between actions of significance and consequence. "Moral value" implies responsibility for the choice.

2. Glaucon versus Socrates. Put the question: Would you be honest about something if there were no chance in the world that you could be detected doing the dishonest thing?

3. Commentators have for centuries questioned whether Socrates' argument that the just man values the just act for its own sake is either rational or realistic.

4. Point out to the class that Socrates was also convinced that no evil can befall a good man. How do they feel about this?

5. The rational view--that to know the good is sufficient--has historically been in conflict with the view that people act out of self-interest. Can people reasonably be expected to ignore their own concerns when it comes to moral choice?

6. The Golden Rule as a foundation for much religious morality. Question: Is altruism, or a form of self-interest, really behind it?

7. The public moral conscience. Fear of what others will say. Is this a good check on our behavior? Or an unnecessary restraint?

8. "Morality is all too frequently what other people do wrong," so says the text. How much truth is there in this statement?

9. Unexamined assumptions, which can underlie moral choice, can be found in characteristic statements prefaced by "Of course . . ."

10. How many popular slogans can the class suggest which have influenced the moral values of others (not on their own, of course!)?

11. Moral attitudes toward work. Question: Is work still considered good in our society? Or is the good identified only with the products one can buy with money? Question: How does our society tend to evaluate those who possess material goods in abundance without having worked for them?

12. Discuss the lifeboat quandary in the context not only of situational morality, but the other moral philosophies presented in the chapter. In particular, is the anguish of the ship's captain the anguish of Abraham?

13. Clarifying one's own moral values by contrasting the "should" and the "would."

CHECK LIST OF POINTS OR DISCUSSION TOPICS FROM VIDEOTAPES

I. The Ring of Gyges

A. Story of the magic ring, and its source in Plato, should be pinpointed at the outset.

Updated version in Tolkein recognizable to many students.

B. The narrator and the nurseryman:

1. Fear that the nurseryman was really not blind?

2. The amount involved was too small for the "hassle"?

3. Dishonesty would have troubled the narrator's conscience whether he had been detected or not?

4. The narrator, like most people, automatically behaved as social custom conditioned him to behave?

5. The narrator did the "right thing" because it was the "right thing"?

C. Question asked of the three guests: Is morality inborn--that is, in some way natural to humankind--or must moral values be instilled in people?

D. Questions asked of the Catholic priest:

1. How do you view the moral issue?

2. If the knowledge of right and wrong comes from God, what is the vehicle that delivers this knowledge?

3. What happens if and when the moral values of society conflict with those which supposedly come from God?

4. Is virtue its own reward?

E. Questions asked of the psychologist:

1. Do you agree with Glaucon's position that people do what is right for fear of what people will say if they don't?

2. Does it matter why people do the right thing? (e.g., Even if their hearts are not in it?)

3. If all behavior can be conditioned, does this give the conditioner too much power?

4. (RE: NASA's plans to populate space colonies.) Won't it be tempting for behavioral engineers to be called in to design a perfect society?

5. Doesn't much of the confusion lie in the fact that behavioral reinforcements come from so many sources?

F. Questions asked of the Black Studies coordinator:

1. Is morality a product of the white establishment?

2. (If this is the case), is it better for people to play the game as it is, or try to change the rules?

3. Do you agree with Marx that money is at the heart of moral problems?

4. Thrasymachus, in The Republic, says that moral standards are whatever is in the best interest of the controlling power. One assumes this means the controlling power has to manipulate the others in order to maintain these standards. Is manipulation ever justified?

II. The Anguish of Abraham

A. It helps to let students know in advance that the opening segment (teaser) of the film represents a dramatization of Kierkegaard's phrase--which also gives the program its title.

B. Traditionally, the story of Abraham embodies the quintessence of faith. Kierkegaard: Faith is a leap from uncertainty to commitment.

C. Some reasons for Kierkegaard's obscurity in the 19th century:

1. Ideal of progress (in America, Manifest Destiny) was sharply opposed to Kierkegaard's premise of life's absurdity.

2. 19th century lived in terms of big abstractions: empire, New World, big business, Industrial Revolution, etc. Kierkegaard's insistence on the existential moment would have seemed meaningless.

D. Revival of Kierkegaard in post-war Paris.

1. War meant toppling of many huge abstractions.

2. In a shattered world, what was left except for the individual to carve his or her own destiny?

E. Structure of film (flashing back and forth from Edouard to Abraham) illustrates existential rejection of the historical point of view. There is only the moment.

F. Parallel between Edouard's and Abraham's choices.

1. Edouard: faith in himself and chosen life-style.

2. Abraham: faith in God and chosen religion.

G. Their anguish, having chosen.

1. Edouard: What if my decision costs my brother his life?

2. Abraham: What if there is no God?

H. How each achieves authenticity:

1. Edouard: by accepting the guilt.

2. Abraham: by a willingness to accept any consequences of his faith.

TEACHING ALTERNATIVES

Text

1. People cannot think clearly about their own moral values and those of others without being able to detect value assumptions behind what they or others do and say. A good exercise in value assumptions is to have the class members comb newspapers and magazines for short articles, headlines, and commercials, bringing in some pertinent examples with a few lines about the assumptions underlying each one. Examples to suggest:

   a. "If you have only one life to live, live it as a blonde."

   b. CONVICTED MURDERER FINALLY KEEPS DATE WITH CHAIR.

2. As an exercise in testing out the Golden Rule, this one has proved most effective. Classes enjoy doing it, and the summing up after the game brings very significant feelings and thoughts to light.

   Task: In order to test the Golden Rule, divide into two large groups--one composed of Positive people and the other, Negative. Criterion for admission to either group is your basic life-orientation. Do you try to make other people happy? Or do you tend to shy away from much contact with others on the grounds that most people don't deserve acts of kindness?

   Once the groups have been established, a Positive person seeks out a Negative person, with the idea of giving him/her positive feedback, and saying things guaranteed to please. The Negative person listens, accepts the feedback, and then reciprocates with negative, even hostile, feedback. (Although everyone will be expecting the exchange, and though everyone basically knows it's a game, negative feedback is hard to take on _any_ level.)

   The community discussion after the exchange of feedback should provide quite a learning experience.

The Ring of Gyges

1. Show only half the film (nurseryman episode, and narrator's summation of the story of Gyges). Then select or accept a

panel from the class to react to the moral issues involved, discussing the alternatives.

2. Divide into small groups, charging each to develop an original version of the Gyges story, making certain they do not disturb the point of the original. The new versions can be acted out, as in the film, or else a spokesperson for the group can present the situation to the rest of the class, along with specific questions such as "In this case, did the person act out of Socratic motives or did he illustrate the truth of Glaucon's argument?"

The Anguish Of Abraham

1. The basic principles of existentialism can be taught very quickly, using the ABC method:

   A. absurdity (recognition of basic fact of living)
      abandonment (one realizes one's aloneness)
      anxiety (one wonders where to turn)
      anguish (one never knows whether one's choices were sound)

   B. boredom (so many things seem so meaningless)

   C. crisis (one reaches the "point of no return"--one must give up or find a solid basis for going on)
      commitment (despite the anguish of choice, one transcends absurdity by creating one's own essence)

2. Like Divine Discontent, the title of this film can have multiple personal meanings. Each student can be asked to write a short paper illustrating his or her own anguish on a number of occasions, and indicating what commitment was made. The papers can be handed in for extra credit. Before the end of the period, have people pair off and share with each other what they have written.

JOURNAL TOPICS

1. If you were taking a closed-book test and, looking up, saw someone cheating, what would your reaction be? Why? Would you take any direct action? Why? Why not?

2. In the text Overview to Chapter 5, there is given the example of the man who corrected his underpriced restaurant bill. Is the issue one of moral integrity, or the insignificant amount of money involved?

3. Much is said nowadays about the lack of uniform moral values, and the moral confusion in which young people grow to maturity. What is the reason for the lack of uniformity? Is it desirable to have uniformity? Where would it come from?

4. If, as has been suggested, morality begins in the home, what happens to someone who has been given a moral upbringing only to find that society as a whole is hypocritical about morality? That it is the clever people, not the good people, who get ahead?

5. Should you do unto others as you would have them do unto you, even if they don't?

6. Is the death penalty a just and logical form of punishment? Does it have impact on moral behavior?

7. Is Hemingway's pronouncement that "moral is what you feel good after" a substantial basis for a morality?

8. Can you trace some of the influences of "Of course . . ." on your life and values?

9. Discuss some of the popular slogans which have influenced your own moral values, or at least some of the assumptions behind them.

10. Both lifeboat stories--that of the ship's captain and that of the two men and the dying boy--are true. As a member of each jury, how would you have voted? Why?

11. Describe situational morality in your own words. Does it represent the ideal moral system for our age and our kind of society? Why, or why not?

12. Do you agree with the existential belief that "to be human is to be authentic"?

13. Do you note a significant difference between the "should" and the "would" in your own value system? Give examples.

MODULAR INTERIOR STRUCTURE

The two programs fall into a nicely contrasting relationship. The Ring of Gyges presents the overview--a consideration of the motives behind moral behavior. First, why did the narrator not cheat the blind man? Second, which of the three guests comes closest to realism in assessing the basis of moral behavior: the priest, who believes morality comes from God; the psychologist, who believes people can be conditioned to behave as we would wish; or the professor, who believes both conditioning and an innate (categorical) sense of right and wrong exist?

The Anguish of Abraham delineates a specific moral philosophy predicated on the assumption that moral behavior stems from a commitment to authenticity.

If the instructor wishes to relate one film to the other, perhaps it would be profitable to carry the idea of authenticity back to The Ring of Gyges, and have the class consider whether any of the positions illustrated or expressed are based on a commitment to or even a need for authenticity.

ESSAY QUESTIONS

I. Text

1. What is a moral value? Mention any three sources of moral values.

2. Which one gives the more persuasive argument--Socrates or Glaucon?

3. If there is someone cheating on this test right now, what do you intend to do about it? Why?

4. With which moral position discussed anywhere in the module are you most sympathetic? Why?

5. Illustrate how the phrase "Of course . . ." can help you to clarify your own moral values.

6. Mention two things you generally believe people <u>should</u> do and two things, in contrast, you believe you personally <u>would</u> do. Why the difference?

7. Is the Golden Rule, in your opinion, a solid basis for social morality? Why, or why not?

II. <u>The Ring Of Gyges</u>

1. Briefly but concisely, what is the real moral issue in the story of the narrator's encounter with the nurseryman?

2. What would you do if a blind shopkeeper handed you a wallet and asked you to make your own change? Why would you do this?

3. Identify the moral position of each of the panelists. To which one are you most sympathetic? Why?

III. <u>The Anguish Of Abraham</u>

1. Complete this statement in a paragraph: "If I were Edouard, and my friends tried to convince me I was not responsible for my brother's death, I would . . ."

2. Kierkegaard supposed that Abraham must have experienced anguish at the thought of having to sacrifice his son. Would a devout believer agree?

3. What is meant by the narrator's statement, "God is Abraham's personal truth"?

4. Define "authentic" as simply as possible, but in purely existential terms.

SURVEY 2 PRESCRIPTIONS

Answers

2 1. Those who responded to #1, 3, 4, or 5 receive the prescription:

> In the film, The Anguish of Abraham, Edouard realizes that his brother has a choice. Against the protests of his friends, he chooses to accept sole responsibility for his brother's death; in that choice he achieves authenticity as a human being, for he refuses to blame other people or circumstances for what has happened.

4 2. Those who responded #1, 2, 3, or 5 receive the prescription:

> Improvisation is the art of leaving a set musical theme behind and taking flight. The improvisation can either be written into the score by the composer, or left to the discretion of the performer. As both Jazz and Bach prove, improvisation can be successful only when it springs naturally from a controlled and disciplined musical form.

1 3. Those who responded #2, 3, 4, or 5 receive the prescription:

> The apparently free motion of the kite is a direct result of the tight grasp of those who are holding it. This would symbolize the moral discipline which alone permits the freedom of the authentic human being.

5 4. Those who responded #1, 2, 3, or 4 receive the prescription:

> The first four reasons are all given by the narrator. The stem of the question asks for the best reason. Since all of the first four are given, number five is the best.

Answers

2 5. Those who responded #1, 3, 4, or 5 receive the prescription:

> The essence of Socratic moral philosophy is that one does the right thing because it is the right thing--not because one profits from doing it. Self-interest is the very last motive the rational person could possibly have.

4 6. Those who responded #1, 2, 3, or 5 receive the prescription:

> In the opinion of many, Plato's Republic is the single most important work of philosophy ever penned. One reason surely is the number of subjects treated. The dialogs include discussions on education, love, art, and the nature of the beautiful. But the transcendent theme of the whole work is justice. To Plato, justice is the quality of the good embodied in government. In other words, the subject of the book is what constitutes the perfect, the most rational organization of society.

2 7. Each incorrect response receives a prescription:

(1) Whether there can be universal ethical laws is not really questioned in Glaucon's story of The Ring of Gyges. The point, rather, is that people behave morally not because ethical laws are universal, but because they are afraid of losing their reputations by violating such laws.

(3) A superficial reading of the story of Gyges may cause some to believe it demonstrates "might makes right," because Gyges owns a powerful ring. But Glaucon does not insist the shepherd's actions are right--only that, if no one were watching, people would not behave morally.

(4) The story of Abraham belongs to the Old Testament, not to Plato's Republic. You probably recalled having read about Abraham in connection with existential morality.

Answers

(5) This is the position taken by Socrates, who argued that a good man will do the just thing, no matter whether he loses his reputation for it or not. The point of Glaucon's story of the ring, of course, is that people behave morally only because society is watching, and they fear for their good name.

3 8. Those who responded #1, 2, 4, or 5 receive the prescription:

To restate Glaucon's story in up-to-date, more realistic terms, the script writers substituted the blindness of the nurseryman for Gyge's invisibility. No one could really become invisible, but there are many situations in which one could escape detection for wrongdoing. Glaucon's point is still very pertinent.

5 9. Those who responded #1, 2, 3, or 4 receive the prescription:

Kierkegaard is really not discussing the historical Abraham, whose motives he would not have presumed to know, or about what the Old Testament implies concerning Abraham. Kierkegaard is using Abraham as a symbol of all people who act on the faith that what they are doing is right, and who can never be certain their faith is well-founded. For Kierkegaard, most of the beliefs underlying human actions are rooted in faith of one kind or another. Anguish is the price all of us must pay for making a choice. There never can be certainty that the choice is the best one we could have made.

2 10. Those who responded #1, 3, 4, or 5 receive the prescription:

Sartre, an atheistic existentialist, believes that humanity must first come to terms with its nothingness. "Nothing" here means having no purpose, or any preordained essence. Humanity is an accidental eruption on the planet--nothing more. But once people recognize this fact, they can discover they are free to conceive and control their own destinies.

Answers

1 11. Those who responded #2, 3, 4, or 5 receive the prescription:

> Hemingway once said that moral "is what you feel good after." While this pronouncement can hardly be considered philosophical in any formal sense of the word, it is close enough to situationalism for us to say that, based on this famous remark, Hemingway's outlook would relate morality to people and situations. It appears to be as far from absolutism as a viewpoint can get.

3 12. Those who responded #1, 2, 4, or 5 receive the prescription:

> In the debate with Socrates, Glaucon insists that people refrain from wrong actions only because they fear being caught and losing their reputations. Glaucon then asks Socrates whether an eminently just man who is wrongly imprisoned for crimes he did not commit can still act virtuously if he has a reputation for dishonesty. The just man, Glaucon asserts, acts from the same motive as the unjust--that is, his good name in the community.

1 13. Those who responded #2, 3, 4, or 5 receive the prescription:

> The terms are all important in the deliberation of existentialists. Authentic, as the existentialist uses the word, means totally consistent from every vantage point. An authentic person's actions are consistent with his beliefs. An example of inauthentic conduct would be a person committing a cruel act in a religious cause.

2 14. Those who responded #1, 3, 4, or 5 receive the prescription:

> The disappearing man is meant to remind us of Gyges himself, the shepherd who found the ring in Glaucon's legend in Plato's <u>Republic</u>. Visibility, then, comes to symbolize the outward appearance of virtue. It is important to be visually virtuous, but the question is whether the narrator is invisibly virtuous as well.

Answers

4 15. Those who responded #1, 2, 3, or 5 receive the prescription:

> Both jazz and Bach share one thing--the fashioning of a kind of music that begins with a strict discipline and then liberates itself from that discipline. The narrator makes a comparison between that music and the ongoing drive in humanity to liberate itself.

4 16. Those who responded #1, 2, 3, or 5 receive the prescription:

> In the text, melody is defined as "significant repetition of sounds," but because romantic music of the nineteenth century defined "significant" as appealing to the pleasure centers of listeners, it was sensuous repetition that became significant--a repetition of selected sounds that had been proved as most pleasurable. Many contemporary composers, however, are returning to a more basic definition of melody.

2 17. Those who responded #1, 3, 4, or 5 receive the prescription:

> The tipoff word here is "numerical." Jeremy Bentham is identified with the Hedonic Calculus, through which one decided on the moral appropriateness (or lack of it) of an action by assigning plus numerical values to pleasure, and minus values to pain. Critics have not taken Bentham's proposals very seriously.

1 18. Those who responded #2, 3, 4, or 5 receive the prescription:

> The hint was contained in the words "clearly prescribed." Of the options given, Judeo-Christian morality is the one that is based on law, on the Commandments. Since one may not steal, Judeo-Christian morality could not approve of the man's breaking into the pharmacy--no matter how deplorable it might find the pharmacist's profiteering.

Answers

4 19. Those who responded #1, 2, 3, or 5 receive the prescription:

The situationalist looks as objectively as possible at all sides in a moral issue. He or she takes both motives and consequences into account. A situationalist would have a hard time with this one, since the immorality of the pharmacist's price-gouging would be as bad as, if not worse than, breaking and entering. Still, it is hard to condone theft as the solution to a problem.

5 20. Those who responded #1, 2, 3, or 4 receive the prescription:

The tipoff word here is "reason." Socrates used only reason as his guide, and would surely have argued that, if stealing is wrong in one case, it is wrong in another. Who would wish to live in a society in which stealing is sometimes all right? Where would the line be drawn? Would not many insist that they had as much right to steal as this unfortunate man?

3 21. Those who responded #1, 2, 4, or 5 receive the prescription:

The tipoff word here is "painful." The husband would have to weigh two wrongs against each other. If he allowed his wife to die, what would his conscience do to him? If he broke into the pharmacy, he would not only be going against a moral principle ingrained in most of us, but he would be vulnerable to being caught and possibly jailed. All the existentialist could recommend is that he ponder the choice carefully, then make a commitment to what he honestly believes is the best course of action, with another commitment to take the consequences.

3 22. Those who responded #1, 4, or 5 receive the prescription:

"Future Shock" is a psychological sense of displacement and alienation as a consequence of too much change happening too fast. One of the symptoms of the condition is noise addiction--a result of overstimulation from information overload. People suffer a reverse reaction--instead of seeking quiet, they demand more and more sound.

Those who responded #2 receive the prescription:

The correct answer is information overload, but your choice of Option 2 deserves a comment. It is true that, if you were addicted to noise, you would resist silence. But noise addiction, according to Toffler, is a symptom--not the cause of the problem. Information overload, as a result of rapid changes in society, causes overstimulation, which in turn causes noise addiction, which in turn leads one to reject solitude and silence.

1 23. Those who responded #2, 3, 4, or 5 receive the prescription:

A fugue is characterized by the simultaneous interplay of two or more melodic lines. The form, characterized by a general love of ornamentation and complexity, was a great favorite of J. S. Bach and other composers of the Baroque era. The Bach fugues are among the richest multidimensional musical sounds ever conceived.

5 24. Each incorrect response receives a prescription:

(1) Flamboyance is generally a negative term in reference to an artist's work. To be sure, many composers and performers can display flamboyance, but not in their most profound moments. One could hardly suppose that jazz musicians would be attracted to Bach for his most superficial qualities. Actually, none of the options is applicable to the question.

(2) The brook, river, and ocean sequence is applicable to the film "Jazz/Bach," not the composer himself. None of the options given is really pertinent.

(3) Percussive effects as such come later than Bach in the history of Western music. Baroque music is characterized by complexity, especially polyphony,

the simultaneous playing of different themes, not percussion. None of the options is really pertinent.

(4) Since improvisation is the very soul of jazz, it hardly seems likely that jazz musicians would prefer Bach's formalism to his very prevalent use of improvisation. None of the options cited is really pertinent.

3 25. Those who responded #1, 2, 4, or 5 receive the prescription:

Most symphonies open with a sonata movement, which is characterized by the presentation of two themes, their development through elaborations of varying sorts, and finally a restatement (recapitulation) of them in the original form. A monochord is the name given to an ancient stringed instrument used by the Greeks and other early societies.

5 26. Those who responded #1, 2, 3, or 4 receive the prescription:

A musical theme, as Westerners generally understand the term, is an arrangement of tones in a particular kind of sequence that is clearly distinguishable from what precedes and follows. We can thus say that it is a musical parallel to human individualism.

4 27. Those who responded #1, 2, 3, or 5 receive the prescription:

A sculpture, which is three-dimensional, cannot be experienced unless it stands free in an open space. Similarly, musical notes and melodies require a context of silence in order to be heard for what they are. Of course, some contemporary music, notably certain forms of rock, seem to keep going without significant pause, so that the distinction between the sounds is often blurred. While I would not necessarily insist that rock is not true music, I think its unceasing motion will be considered a pecularity of our age--not a profound change in the character of music itself.

Answers

1 28. Each incorrect response receives a prescription:

(2) Since much of our cultural heritage is embodied in folk music, a revival of this art could hardly mean a rejection of that heritage. Rather, folk music, which could often be sung by the whole group, brought the young people together and helped them to ward off feelings of alienation and fragmentation.

(3) I would agree that the youth culture of the 1960's often sought religious experience, but I cannot agree that folk music is characterized by religious themes. Indeed, many folk songs reflect a very tragic view of existence in a godless universe. But what much folk music has in common is that it can be sung by people in groups, helping them to ward off feelings of alienation and fragmentation.

(4) Like all earlier songs, folk music is not especially free of sexist attitudes. One could hardly imagine looking to folk music for nonsexist sentiments. The youth culture of the 1960's loved folk music because it could be sung in groups, helping young people to ward off feelings of alienation and fragmentation.

(5) The revival of folk music in the 1960's was attributed, at least in part, to young people's need to ward off feelings of alienation and fragmentation. What they liked about folk songs was that these could be sung in groups, creating a communal spirit.

5 29. Those who responded #1, 3, or 4 receive the prescription:

Since music at least in one sense is defined as the external anchor of our feelings, one can say that listening to only one kind of music all the time is to externalize only particular feelings, hence, to know only one side of one's personality. Such narrowness is a way of life, and keeping many emotions unexplored. Since all three options are correct, the best response to this question is Option 5.

Answers

Those who responded #2 receive the prescription:

Doubtless, many people who fall in love with one kind of music believe they possess a fine critical discernment, but the truly appreciative critic of music is open to new forms of musical stimulation. Those who stay with their favorite, to the exclusion of everything else, know only one side of their personality, keep many emotions unexplored, and certainly emulate Woodrow Tatlock, for whom narrowness was a way of life. Option 5 contains all three of these statements.

1 30. Each incorrect response receives a prescription:

(2) The freedom referred to is freedom within the music. Even so, there is no evidence that jazz musicians are known as a group for battling social prejudice. In music, they liberate themselves only after they have mastered their art.

(3) The improvisation (freedom) is often written into the score, but it gets into the score only after the artist has achieved mastery of the form. It is not the writing down of the music in itself which constitutes the artist's freedom.

(4) It is hard to insist upon a relationship between freedom and proficiency in more than one instrument. One can achieve musical freedom with one instrument, but whatever the case, freedom is always a consequence of discipline, and the mastery of form. It is never a random thing; otherwise, we leave the realm of music.

(5) A musician could have an open attitude toward all types of music and still be tied down to the exact notes of every score he or she plays. Musical freedom means going beyond the score, but before this can occur, the musician must attain mastery of his art.

Answers

2 31. Those who responded #1, 3, 4, or 5 receive the prescription:

> The brook is the most confined body of water, and would represent the most disciplined kind of music. The river represents more freedom, but it is still held within bounds. The ocean is the most unconstrained of the three and thus symbolizes improvisational flights of fancy. The idea is that one cannot start with ocean in the quest for liberation; one must start with the brook.

MODULE V

PHILOSOPHY: FAITH AND SCIENCE

TEACHING OVERVIEW

The amount of material available in this module suggests that a major choice be made by the instructor at the outset. One direction in which to take the student is to contrast the meaning of faith and the meaning of rational certainty, perhaps reaching the conclusion that a balance between the two is essential to human growth. To believe only what science and reason can certify is perhaps to close one's mind to alternate visions of reality. To spend one's lifetime seeking only transcendent truths, on the other hand, is possibly to run the risk of displacement in an age mainly built by science and its primary instrument, reason.

The other possible direction is to assume that, while the positive achievements of science are undeniable, the religious quest is legitimate and, as *The Outer Circle* indicates, a growing interest in religion exists in many who grew up without religious faith and now find a void within themselves. The second film of the module, *The Problem Of Evil*, addresses itself to questions that are extremely important to people with faith, even to those who are considering a commitment to faith; and the instructor and class can spend a profitable week discussing such matters as how, of if, God exists.

Students who have been raised in a strongly religious home, and who continue to practice within a particular faith, have shown great interest in the perspectives on faith versus reason which this module provides. Students without particular religious affiliations have nonetheless been intrigued by those perspectives, some perhaps coming to the realization that very great minds indeed have pondered profound questions they have hitherto been ignoring or putting aside.

Whichever direction one takes, the module should demonstrate one overriding theme: science can do and know many things faith thought impossible, but faith has insights that elude the scientist.

CHECK LIST OF POINTS OR DISCUSSION TOPICS FROM TEXT

1. Faulkner's "The Bear," and its relevance to the main subject, which is the continuing need people have for what Thoreau called higher truths, and what Tillich called ultimate concerns.

   Note: While the text provides all the information about "The Bear" which students require for an understanding of the point, many students are simply not accustomed to grasping analogies.

2. The idea that early people thought they heard the voices of the gods talking inside them proves stimulating to classes, who are generally not familiar with the left/right hemisphere hypotheses, or at least such an application as this. The theory that these inner voices were really right hemispheres talking to left hemispheres comes from Julian Jaynes's _The Origins of Consciousness in the Breakdown of the Bicameral Mind_, the central thesis of which is that people have not always been directly aware of their inner selves, or that interior activity was not always regarded as something happening in the brain.

   Other left/right hemisphere dichotomies are pertinent here, and the instructor who wishes to pursue them will find more material in Chapter 3 of the text.

3. It may not be necessary to dwell on the achievements of all the Pre-Socratics mentioned, but the significance of Thales's first question in philosophy--What is everything made of?--should be pointed out as the beginning of the schism between accepting without certainty and the quest for demonstrable truth.

4. A convenient and quickly grasped perspective is to show the rise of rational inquiry from Socrates to Augustine, with the latter's putting a halt to it on the grounds that the ultimate mysteries forever evade human understanding.

   Note: It is a simple matter to go from this perspective to The Outer Circle, with its plea for constantly redefining what the ultimate mysteries are and how far the human mind is able to go to penetrate them, and to The Problem Of Evil, with its investigation into the anguish which those mysteries inflict upon even the most devout.

5. The rational arguments for God, set forth by St. Anselm and St. Thomas Aquinas, can excite some classes and bore others. They are provided in the text for those instructors who focus on religion in the module, and whose students display interest in proving (or disproving) religious truths.

6. One cannot overstress to the students the tremendous impact and long-range importance of the Newtonian world view. We are still the children of Newton, despite quantum physics (see Chapter 15) and, earlier, the relativistic universe of Einstein. Newton gave us the concept of nature as a vast, beautifully integrated machine--all parts of which were interlocked through an infallible chain of cause and effect. One might even point out that Einstein was seeking the means of "saving" Newton's uniformity, not destroying it.

7. Swift fits in (another Newtonian derivative!) with the pessimistic reactions to the mechanized universe inherited by the 18th century--a universe from which God, and moral values, had departed.

8. "Dover Beach" and "Ulysses" are two poems which take opposite positions with regard to the promise of science (and perhaps even technology).

9. Kant's separation of critical and practical philosophy is mentioned in the text, but the emphasis is on the practical (or pragmatic) approach to religion. If the need is there, one can easily demonstrate what Kant means by critical philosophy with the philosopher's analysis of time and space as categories of the mind. No one, says Kant, really has to teach us what time and space are--but we do not observe them with the senses either. Our minds have a fundamental grasp of them because they are categories with which we are born.

10. William James's pragmatic approach to religion, with its psychological basis. One can legitimately believe when a hypothesis is live, forced, and momentous. Of course, the crucial factor in the hypothesis "God exists" is whether it is forced, or avoidable; the question often stimulates good discussion.

11. Without spending the entire week on the subject of whether there is or is not a legitimate revival of religious concerns on the literary and intellectual horizon, one ought to touch upon the matter. Kubrick's *2001: A Space Odyssey* ties in with Pierre Teilhard de Chardin and, though the film is an astonishing 15 years old, it is still popular on college campuses, and worth discussing.

CHECK LIST OF POINTS OR DISCUSSION TOPICS FROM VIDEOTAPES

I. The Outer Circle

A. The goliards--medieval student priests--rebelling against austerities of the faith, composing and singing robust, sometimes ribald songs, in praise of the Dionysian life. (Song sung by goliard in teaser is an actual medieval lyric, with new musical setting.)

B. Cosmology represented on easel in schoolroom would be the Ptolemaic or geocentric universe.

C. Council of Nicaea, A.D. 325, doctrine of the Trinity becomes dogma. Council of Chalcedon, A.D. 451, doctrine of the Virgin birth becomes dogma.

D. Outer circles: dogma is to the medieval world what scientific positivism is to the modern world. In the first instance, science breaks through the circle--in the second, the uncharted world beyond the circle is a revival of metaphysics and spirituality.

E. Segment on the Scopes Trial creates the opportunity to discuss whether there have been recent controversies over the suppression of certain material or life-styles.

   1. What about the teacher who admitted he was homosexual, and was immediately fired? Is the same principle at work, or a different one?

   2. What about outlawing prayer in the public school? Same principle?

F. Pierre Teilhard de Chardin (1881-1955) important as link between Catholicism and Darwin. Teilhard taught that not only matter but spirit was evolving, and placed a teleological construction on evolution, which would culminate in the emergence of the Super Christ.

G. How many interests and practices of the present generation represent legitimate forays beyond the outer circle? Meditation? Yoga? TM? Eckankar? Divine Light Mission? Etc., etc.

II. The Problem Of Evil

A. It helps to point out even before the film that there are three principle kinds of evil involved: physical, moral, and natural. The death of the young wife would represent physical evil (or what some people would consider to be so); the genocide attempted by Nazi Germany would represent moral evil; and Moby Dick (as well as hurricanes, earthquakes, etc.) would represent natural evil.

B. On the death of the wife: students in the pilot test enjoyed discussing the reason people like to allocate blame when an unexpected tragedy occurs.

C. What are the religious explanations possible?

   1. The wife was free to place her life in jeopardy?

   2. The wife was predestined to die at that moment?

3. The husband or wife was being punished?

4. God had reasons which humankind cannot comprehend?

5. God had no reasons; since He is all-powerful, God cannot be bound by reasons?

D. Mysticism - the acceptance of paradox without question; with no tension between the possible and the impossible.

E. Spinoza - evil as illusion. Since God is all things, what we call evil is an attribute of God--hence he cannot be called evil.

F. Candide - satire on the evil-denying optimism of the period.

Question: What is Voltaire recommending in place of Pangloss's resolute optimism? If there is no God (as there is not for Voltaire), can there be evil to accept? Or must one accept the random nature of things? But how random are the indignities inflicted on Candide?

G. Bill's final conclusion--perhaps he has not begun to ask the right questions. What may some of these be?

1. Does the question "Why does God permit evil?" beg the question?

2. Is there ever an appropriate (or inappropriate) time to die?

3. May asking why God allows this and not that be a denial of freedom of the will?

TEACHING ALTERNATIVES

Text

1. Divide the class into two main groups--those who advocate faith, and those for whom science is the primary method for discovering the truth. If the group sizes are too unwieldy, break the main groupings into smaller units.

Ask participants on either side to discuss questions like:

a. Is science getting close to explaining the physical origins of the universe?

b. Have modern investigations into the age and size of the universe diminished the cause of religion?

c. Is it likely that life exists on other planets? If there were life, how might this fact fit in with biblical views?

d. Does the place and function of religion in contemporary society need redefining?

Then assemble the entire class, and share some of the views which have come to light.

2. Ask students to study the arguments of Anselm and Aquinas in detail, and then come to class prepared to do one of the following:

   a. Add a new argument to the list.

   b. Question the logic of one of the arguments.

   c. Defend the logic of one of the arguments.

   Note: If there are students who defended and students who attacked the same argument, a debating situation immediately arises.

The Outer Circle

1. Ask students to come to class with two sheets of paper. On one there should be a list of current "outer circles" (e.g., the course; the school; the law; police; parents). On the other, a parallel list of alternatives (e.g., turning children over to the state when they are born, instead of having them raised by their parents).

   These lists can be shared and debated in small groups.

   Variation: Assign an "outer circle" authority to each group. Charge the group members to take the goliard's approach, which must then be countered in each instance by the authority person's arguments in favor of "holding the circle." After a time, share some of the more explosive debates.

2. Ask each student to compose a short poem, beginning with the words "They tell me that . . .", and come to class ready to read it to the others.

The Problem Of Evil

The history of evil (or the belief in evil) has traditionally uncovered a dichotomy between moral and physical evil. The death of the young wife in the film can be taken as physical evil. The Holocaust is cited as a tragic example of moral evil.

Divide the class into two groups. Group A is to assume that evil is simply a word without objective reference. Group B is to assume that moral evil is a reality that unfortunately exists outside subjective interpretations of the world. Group A is to discuss the real nature of that which has been called moral evil, while Group B is to come up with reasons for believing that moral evil does indeed exist.

JOURNAL TOPICS

1. Read carefully the Chapter 8 opening account of Faulkner's "The Bear." What does the bear represent to you? Are there "bears" in your own belief system?

2. We are told that early societies accepted as rulers or holy persons those who claimed to hear the voices of the gods. Have we a modern equivalent of these inner voices as criteria for leadership?

3. Make a list of statements beginning with the words "There is no doubt in my mind that . . ." Select the five most provocative ones and put them in your Journal, along with an explanation of the source of your certainty.

4. If you are a religious person, discuss any two questions you have which you believe your religion cannot answer. Or, two questions which atheists often raise--and which your religion can answer.

5. Of the six arguments for God's existence presented in the text, which strikes you as the most convincing? Give your reasons. (Alternate version: Which strikes you as the least convincing?)

6. Where do most religions stand now on the theory of evolution? Is Darwin totally accepted? Mainly accepted? Half-and-half?

7. Summarize two of St. Augustine's difficulties with the account of creation as presented in Genesis. In your opinion, is faith a satisfactory answer to these questions?

8. Does religion, in your opinion, seem to stress faith in paradox, and the inexplicable mysteries, or the certainty of its teachings and moral requirements?

9. Can one be primarily scientific in one's outlook and still be religious in certain aspects? Or is either orientation an all-or-nothing proposition?

10. If there is moral evil in the world, does it spring from disobedience to God? If there is no God, can there be moral evil? If there is no moral evil, can we condemn what others do?

11. Bill, the hero of The Problem Of Evil, decides he may be asking the wrong questions. What does he mean? What are some questions he could ask?

MODULAR INTERIOR STRUCTURE

Certainty and faith set up a natural yin/yang structure. One is certain that airplane travel is perfectly safe; on the other hand, one must have faith that the mechanics know their job, that the pilot has his or her mind on the work, etc. If one must have faith in one's certainty, there must also be a certainty about one's faith--a resolute commitment to it.

The yin/yang between closing and opening the outer circle can also structure the entire week. One can use The Outer Circle to establish the parameters of the module, and then show The Problem Of Evil as possibly an example of difficulties people have had with faith, and an explanation of why some reject the religious in favor of the rational or scientific view of existence.

One or the other film can even be omitted, depending upon whether the instructor wants to emphasize faith versus science as a motif, or complexities within faith itself.

ESSAY QUESTIONS

I. Text

1. Is there a bear in your belief system? What is your bear? Why do you allow it to live?

2. Give two examples of times in which you are sure it is the right brain hemisphere you are experiencing.

3. Can you have religion without God? Can you have God without religion?

4. Plato made a distinction between knowledge and belief. Would you be willing to say that in our time knowledge belongs to science, while religion is a matter of belief?

5. Restate one of the arguments for God in your own words.

6. Which argument for God's existence impressed you the most? Why?

7. Do you agree that there is a considerable revival of religion in our time? If there is, is it a profound one? If you disagree, indicate your reason.

II. The Outer Circle

1. What is an outer circle, as this phrase is used in the film title?

2. Are you happier inside or outside circles?

3. What is the significance of the fact that the young medieval student reappears in the final sequence?

4. Do you think the Church had an alternative in Galileo's case? Should the Church have allowed the scientist an opportunity to speak freely about his beliefs?

5. Complete the following in a short paragraph: "I believe teachers (should, should not) be allowed to advocate any belief whatsoever in class . . ."

III. The Problem Of Evil

1. Restate in your own words what problem(s) evil has posed for theologians and believers.

2. How did St. Augustine cope with the problem of evil?

3. If the husband in the film had not been religious, would his reaction to the death of his wife have been different? Explain.

4. Do you think the husband is still religious at the end of the film? Explain.

5. The priest seems to be troubled by the same questions that Bill has been asking. Do you think it is possible to have doubts, and still be a priest?

6. What does Bill mean when he suggests he might have been trying to spell G-O-D with the wrong blocks? Are there other (right) blocks?

MODULE VI

PHILOSOPHY: EASTERN/WESTERN CONSCIOUSNESS

TEACHING OVERVIEW

The third philosophy unit of the course can be sharply focused--can be, in fact, narrowed down to a very simple premise: don't assume that your way of thinking and of interpreting events is the only one possible. That is, it *sounds* simple upon first hearing but, if one reflects a moment on the matter, one realizes that the most difficult thing any of us can do is try to think like somebody else.

In order to encourage the act of empathy on the students' part, the module centers on the contrast between typically Western and typically Eastern outlooks. The text chapter compares value systems. It attempts to be highly selective without over-simplifying. The West stresses individualism, achievement, upward mobility, possessions status, and power. The East stresses peace and detachment. The West is goal-oriented--the East is wisdom-oriented. The West excludes the many, singles out the great, and venerates the super-achievers. The East includes all, would recommend humility for the great, and venerates the obscure.

Territory And Space examines the contrast within an American family. The young son rejects the territorialism of his father and ancestors. He is not driven by the ideal of success. Instead, he practices Buddhist meditation, much to the displeasure of his parents, who fear that he will "never make anything of himself." The Still And Empty Center follows another young American in his quest for fulfillment. This young man believes it will come in the form of Buddhist enlightenment, but he seeks it on Western terms. He will be super enlightened. He will be dazzling in his detachment. Of course, he fails--at least, at first. He reaches maturity only when he sees that enlightenment means learning to exist directly and simply in the moment, without epic dreams of success. With the realization comes also a simple acceptance of who he is and what he does.

It is not the intention of this module to persuade students that the Eastern way is the way of salvation, but to make as fair a presentation of Eastern modes of consciousness as possible. The viewpoints expressed by the narrators of the films are Buddhist in character, but they are not necessarily the viewpoints of the course. Some students in the pilot test reacted negatively to those narrators, insisting that there was much to be said in favor of the Western way of life. Such critical responses are healthy, and greatly to be encouraged.

CHECK LIST OF POINTS OR DISCUSSION TOPICS FROM TEXT

1. As a religion, Buddhism differs from Christianity, Judaism,

and Islam in that it has no principle of godhead. Buddhism is a way of approaching life based on the disciplined practice of meditation and following the ethical teachings of the Buddha, who was neither a prophet nor a savior, but an enlightened human being.

2. Buddhism differs from Hinduism in the following ways:

   a. In Hinduism, the universe is the outer form of Brahman, an absolute soul; in Buddhism, there is no such thing as absolute identity--there is only egolessness.

   b. Hindus believe that one will attain nirvana, release from suffering, only after many lifetimes; Buddhists believe that nirvana is attainable for some in a single lifetime through an intensive devotion to sitting practice.

   c. In Hinduism, karma is the accumulated debts of one's lifetime that have to be paid off the next time around; in Buddhism, karma is the alternation of cause and effect--the futile merry-go-round of living from which one seeks detachment.

3. Tibetan Buddhism deemphasizes the life and teachings of the Buddha; stresses the importance of the discipline of sitting, especially in a community of meditators, and the necessity of working with a _guru_ or teacher, who is the meditator's major link with the Buddhist tradition; and maintains that Buddha-mind is not only attainable within one lifetime, but may be achieved by more than one Buddha in any era.

4. Zen Buddhism is a tradition of Buddhist practice which originated in China, but has been developed mainly in Japan. Its meditators spend long hours sitting, and frequently live in monastic simplicity. A prominent feature of its teachings is the cryptic parable, concealing the Buddhist message behind a wry smile.

5. The Dharma in Buddhism is the essentially moral structure underlying all existence. One perceives the Dharma through meditation. By transcending the illusion of ego, one's basic intelligence is allowed to function, and one always behaves appropriately.

6. In Buddhism, compassion is not construed in a strictly charitable or humanitarian sense. It means that, having meditated

to the point at which one's own thought processes become clear, one is able to understand why others do what they do. Buddhist compassion is an extremely thorough form of empathy.

CHECK LIST OF POINTS OR DISCUSSION TOPICS FROM VIDEOTAPES

I. Territory And Space

A. Title is major metaphor of film.

Territory - in West, ego, individualism, achievement, status, property
Space - in East, egolessness, detachment

B. Father of boy believes competitiveness is natural in humans; the boy contests this point.

If Buddhists are wrong, then compassion becomes folly. Others will always be taking advantage of you.

C. Another contrast between Hinduism and Buddhism:

1. Hindus believe that behind the apparent change and impermanence of the material world (maya), there is the eternal, unchanging world soul (Brahman). Note: a comparison between Platonism and Hinduism is not off target.

2. Buddhism believes change and impermanence are real, are all that exists, are the means by which "it" continually expresses itself. (If you want to define "it" think of the sentence, "It is raining," and then try to define the subject. You'll have "it.")

D. The pioneers were imbued with the desire to possess the land, and to alter it. A good point to debate is whether there can be progress under Buddhism.

E. Allen Ginsberg and Peter Orlovsky, who are interviewed in the film, belonged to the so-called Beat Generation of the 50's. Many in the movement attempted to develop an alternate life-style through drugs, but have since found in Buddhism a saner way of getting there.

Much of Ginsberg's latest poetry is not written down, but is spoken extemporaneously, with the poet often having no previous idea of what is about to come forth. This represents the trust Buddhists place in the intelligence and creativity of the human mind when it is left to its own devices.

II. The Still And Empty Center

A. The circle can be a complicated symbol in Buddhism. Here one may present the symbol simply as an expression of the unity of all existence. This view should be tied in with the segment on grass and water, and the statement "Each blade of grass tells us what the grass is all about." In Buddhism, there is only existence, and all the many forms of "it" are still "it."

B. The center of this circle is "everywhere and nowhere." This means that the essence of any moment is what it is. One is always at the center of things. In the parlance of today's students, one is always where the action is. This view is in sharp contrast with the typical Western idea that one has to go where the action is.

C. Like many Westerners, Michael is dissatisfied with where and what he is. He seeks to identify himself in terms of a remote ideal he cannot even name. His misty goal of peace and contentment is his "still center," but what he has yet to learn (at least according to the Buddhist view of things) is that the center is empty (non-identifiable, in terms of ego or goal).

D. Michael's efforts to meditate are unsuccessful because:

1. He thinks there is a specific goal, and a specific kind of success that can be so identified.

2. He tries too hard to free himself from his thoughts, when the whole point is to allow the mind to go where it will; eventually, meditators come to see all of their thoughts in the same light--*as* thoughts, with no power in themselves to threaten or induce guilt.

E. Michael's enlightenment is far less spectacular than he had at one time hoped. He identifies with his out-breath as he looks with detachment at each object on his desk. He is at last at the still and empty center. He is in the moment exactly as it is.

TEACHING ALTERNATIVES

Students have enjoyed spending part of a class period learning the simple techniques of meditation. These are:

1. Sit cross-legged on the floor--in the lotus position, if possible.

2. The back must be erect, but not stiff.

3. The hands should be relaxed, and allowed to rest in the lap in a comfortable position.

4. The eyes should be open at all times, with the meditator neither taking everything in, nor shutting anything out.

5. One should not try to concentrate on "nothing." The mind should just wander.

6. Meditators will discover right away that, to avoid boredom, their minds will seek entertainment. To "discourage" an excessive preoccupation with a particular memory or anticipation, meditators should keep coming back to a direct awareness of their out-breath. This will create a sharp contrast between what is real, and the fantasy of the mind's thoughts.

7. If one stays at it long enough, the mind-chatter will start to diminish. The habit of identifying with the out-breath will increase, and there will be a gradually heightened sense of being there in the room.

JOURNAL TOPICS

1. What are your own territory requirements? Could you live without a substantial amount of property, money, status, or influence?

2. What would a completely spacious existence be like (using the term in the Buddhist sense of the word)? Do you think it would be satisfying? Of is "satisfying" beside the point?

3. American Buddhists are strongly anti-drugs in their outlook. They believe people who seek altered consciousness through

drugs do not reach a "higher" reality, but abandon reality altogether. Still, they do speak about altered consciousness through meditation. In what sense do you think they use these terms?

4. Buddhists do not say that ego is bad; they say flatly that ego does not exist. What is this inner sense of "me-ness" we all seem to have?

5. Would those who practice Buddhist meditation all of their lives ever amount to anything? Be specific.

6. The Buddhist Middle Way exists somewhere between highs and lows. Granted that nobody wants the lows, would you be willing to give up the highs?

7. Explain the steps of the Eightfold Path in your own words.

8. Many Americans become Buddhist practitioners while remaining, like Michael in The Still And Empty Center, within the establishment. What sort of jobs do you think would be most conducive to the Buddhist approach to life? Which ones do you think would be in conflict with it?

MODULAR INTERIOR STRUCTURE

Instructors in the pilot test found that classes were able to accommodate a relaxed, less pronounced structure for this module. It is indeed hard to be Aristotelian about a module primarily centered on Buddhist thought. There is really no aspect of the subject that, if treated fairly and openly, does not open up the entire subject for discussion.

If, however, one is more comfortable with a structured presentation, one may consider the following suggestions:

1. Outline the principles of Hindu thought, then deal with the emergence of the Buddha and the shifted emphases in his teachings.

2. Deal positively with both Western and Eastern values, showing either or both films and asking the class to evaluate honestly the life-styles practiced by the central characters.

3. Present the historical facts of Hinduism, Buddhism, Zen Buddhism, and Tibetan Buddhism. Then deal with the growth of American Buddhism as a philosophical, sociological, and psychological phenomenon. Discuss its possible causes, who is attracted to it, and where you think it may be headed.

ESSAY QUESTIONS

I. Text

1. Distinguish between Hinduism and Buddhism on the matter of self.

2. For the millions who regard Buddhism as a religion, the Buddha is surely a sacred figure--almost a deity. What would the Buddha have said of this?

3. The Buddha taught that life is full of suffering. What is the principle cause of suffering? How may it best be overcome?

4. In your own words, and as simply as possible, what does the Buddhist mean by egolessness?

5. Define karma, samsara, and nirvana, according to Buddhism.

6. What does the Buddhist mean by compassion?

7. In Zen Buddhism, the meditation pillow is black to encourage boredom. Why?

II. Territory And Space

1. Complete this statement in a brief paragraph: "If my child showed no sign of wanting to get ahead in this world, I would . . ."

2. The film indicated a connection between Japanese martial arts and meditation practices. What is that connection?

3. Briefly, what is the principle behind the Japanese martial arts?

4. What if we had a Buddhist president?

5. The Zen parable of Ryokan and the thief concludes with Ryokan's regret that he could not have shared the moonlight with the thief. Try to suggest as simply as possible what this means.

III. The Still And Empty Center

1. The narrator says that Americans are looking for a still center. What does she mean?

2. What is the difference between a still center, and a still and <u>empty</u> center?

3. The narrator says of Michael: "Everything about his life seemed to be postponed." Using this observation as the key, explain briefly just what Michael's problem is.

4. What was Michael hoping to find or accomplish at the Buddhist college?

5. What do you think the other meditators had succeeded in doing that Michael had failed to do?

6. Something happened to turn Michael's life around while he was sitting at the desk in his office. In your own words, what was it?

7. The narrator observes, after the change in Michael: "There at the empty and still center, you are Michael, and you are not Michael." In what sense is he both himself and not himself?

SURVEY 3 PRESCRIPTIONS

Answers

3 1. Those who responded #1, 2, 4, or 5 receive the prescription:

> It comes as quite a shock to many people to discover that the original atomic theory, set forth by Democritus and Leucippus, was in existence long before Plato and Aristotle. The word "atom" itself is Greek and means "something that cannot be cut." Since ultimate reality, reasoned Democritus and Leucippus, was the atom, their system of philosopny acquired the name "materialism" because it asserted that nothing was real except matter. Plato was appalled by this philosophy.

4 2. Those who responded #1, 2, 3, or 5 receive the prescription:

> St. Augustine struggled for a long time to find a meaningful way of accounting for the existence of evil. The source of his problem was the apparent paradox that developed when one recognized that God's omnipotence and moral perfection must somehow coexist with evil. How could God be powerless to prevent evil? How could an all-powerful God allow evil? The absence of good, rather than the presence of an actual force coexisting with God. But this conclusion by no means settled the matter for theologians.

4 3. Those who responded #1, 2, 3, or 5 receive the prescription:

> Fundamentalism is the position adopted by those religions which interpret the Bible literally, rather than symbolically. William Jennings Bryan, the Prosecutor in the Scopes Trial, once sought the presidency, and hoped to influence legislation which would ban Darwin's theory from all public schools. In that trial, the defendants were really Charles Darwin and the theory of evolution.

Answers

4 4. Those who responded #1, 2, 3, or 5 receive the prescription:

Pragmatism developed out of the reaction against pure rationalism as the only acceptable road to philosophical truth. The pragmatists argued that rationalism could "prove" only what was already implied in the definitions of the terms they used. Instead, they wanted a firm base of operations in reality, and demanded that philosophical speculation be concerned with feasibility, workability, function, and the psychological will to believe. As to this last element, the pragmatists maintained that many beliefs, such as that God exists, could not be defended rationally, but were nonetheless undeniable in an individual's psychological reality.

n/a 5. Each response receives a prescription:

(1) As you know, many philosophers have attempted to prove God's existence using logic alone. Their critics argue that those people who accepted this logic were ones disposed to believe in God to begin with. There is no ultimate solution. One cannot say that logic transcends science, when logic is one of the primary tools of the scientist. I guess it's a matter of whose logic one is using. The logic of science needs tangible proof; the logic of religion does not.

(2) Some strict advocates of scientific methods might hold this position, but I doubt that the most eminent scientists would. Einstein, himself, postulated a need for both science and religion. The term "meaningful" is open to a number of interpretations. But in this option, it suggests "absolute." Science is very wary about absolutes.

(3) I think even the most extreme advocates of scientific positivism would agree that humankind possesses certain intuitions, including that of God's existence, which lie outside the domain of logic and science, and which neither require nor are capable of rational proofs.

(4) Here is a most controversial point. Those who accept

revelation as the means whereby God's word is communicated to humankind are often in the position of having to believe literally in certain things that science would say are impossible. Science, of course, can disprove some aspects of revelation, but the devout demonstrate the profundity of their faith by believing that religious truth often transcends natural law.

(5) Are you speaking only for yourself, or for people in general? I think that upon careful inspection you may discover a resurgence of religion today. Possibly you are not in sympathy with such a revival, but you should not ignore it, or the possible reasons which have led to it.

2 6. Each incorrect response receives a prescription:

(1) Your answer is known as the argument from motion. The fifth argument is that, since the universe bears witness to design, there must have been a designer, who is God. A famous challenge to this argument was made by David Hume, who said that design was just an idea inside the human mind.

(3) Your answer is known as the argument from causation. The fifth argument is that, since the universe bears witness to design, there must have been a designer, who is God. A famous challenge to this argument was made by David Hume, who said that design was just an idea inside the human mind.

(4) Your answer is known as the ontological argument. The fifth argument is that, since the universe bears witness to design, there must have been a designer, who is God. A famous challenge to this argument was made by David Hume, who said that design was just an idea inside the human mind.

(5) Your answer is known as the argument from gradation. The fifth argument is that, since the universe bears witness to design, there must have been a designer, who is God. A famous challenge to this argument was made by David Hume, who said that design was just an idea inside the human mind.

Answers

2 7. Those who responded #1, 3, 4, or 5 receive the prescription:

For many hundreds of years, church dogma took the place of philosophy. The exercise of reason was discouraged as unnecessary when one, after all, had faith to live by. But with the rise of scholasticism in the universities during the 11th and 12th centuries, there was a renewed interest in philosophy, especially the use of reason to prove the tenets held by faith.

1 8. Those who responded #2, 3, 4, or 5 receive the prescription:

Teilhard de Chardin is the most prominent of those philosophers who have attempted to reconcile religion with what they consider the incontrovertible facts of science, including the theory of evolution.
He views evolution in terms of spiritual purpose, the gradual emergence of a morally perfected species of being, transcendently embodied in the figure of the Super Christ, who will come when evolution reaches Omega Point.

1 9. Those who responded #2, 3, 4, or 5 receive the prescription:

You may possibly have known the answer. Note that the stem of the question indicated that all of the options were positive about the relationship of Tibetan and Mainstream Buddhism except one. The only negative element was perpetual homage to the one true Buddha. That is, while Mainstream Buddhism tends to focus on the life and teachings of Siddhartha Gautama, Tibetan Buddhism accepts the potential Buddha-hood of all persons.

3 10. Those who responded #1, 2, or 4 receive the prescription:

Many Americans who are now practicing Buddhists were interviewed as part of the research for this module. When asked the fundamental reason for making this choice, most answered that they had become disillusioned by the success/failure orientation of our society. They expressed the belief that, so long as one remained caught up in the prevailing value system, one was forced to judge every turn of fortune in relation to how near or far it was from success. In their estimation, Buddhism has liberated them from such an obsession.

Those who responded #5 receive the prescription:

Your answer may indeed explain the reason some turn to Buddhism. Buddhists themselves say there are no bad motives for turning to sitting meditation as a way of life, but there are unrealistic explanations. Escape is one of them. Buddhism teaches wakefulness, a hard and direct confrontation with reality in order that one may behave appropriately. Most Buddhists interviewed for this module indicated that their reason for adopting the practice was dissatisfaction with the success/failure orientation of our society.

1 11. Those who responded #2, 3, 4, or 5 receive the prescription:

Hinduism taught that one reached enlightenment, nirvana, only after morally perfecting oneself through many, many lifetimes. The Buddha broke with this tradition by asserting that he himself had attained enlightenment in the course of a single lifetime and that, by following the same path, others could do it too.

3 12. Those who responded #1, 2, 4, or 5 receive the prescription:

Christ and Buddha were neither compared nor contrasted in the program. It is not appropriate to assert that any relationship exists, other than that both led exemplary lives and left behind profound ethical teachings. Buddha was in no sense a deity nor the prophet of a deity. He was a mortal person who found the road to tranquility and sought to help others find it as well.

4 13. Those who responded #1, 2, 3, or 5 receive the prescription:

Michael achieves a modest sort of enlightenment--not

the spectacular experience he had hoped to find when he first became involved with Buddhism. He realizes that the state of wakefulness can be found anywhere, even at his desk in the office. He recognized that Buddhism is an approach to what one does, not necessarily a separate form of behavior. One assumes that he will stay at the job without despairing.

4 14. Those who responded #1, 2, 3, or 5 receive the prescription:

In the Hindu trinity, Brahma represents the Creator, or the force of creativity, while Shiva (his opposite) represents the force of destruction, and Vishnu represents the preserver, or the balance between the two.

4 15. Those who responded #1, 2, 3, or 5 receive the prescription:

Critics of Buddhism in the West often point out that people who become accustomed to a high standard of living and the gratification of their desires cannot adjust readily to Buddhist austerity and detachment, though initially they may entertain the delusion that they have liberated themselves. They also maintain that Buddhism works best in underdeveloped countries with a long tradition of poverty and the relative insignificance of the individual. Exponents of Buddhism counter by saying that enlightenment can take place anywhere.

4 16. Those who responded #1, 2, 3, or 5 receive the prescription:

Even the most dedicated exponents of Buddhism in American society urge beginners to expect no miraculous alteration of their lives, and not to overcommit themselves to a practice they may not be able to sustain. Rather, they encourage the beginner to set aside a certain length of time each day for sitting practice. This, they believe, will not interfere with the practitioner's regular routine, nor will it disrupt family and social life. Buddhism, they point out, does not have to mean total withdrawal from active participation in life.

Answers

2 17. Those who responded #1, 3, 4, or 5 receive the prescription:

> Galileo died in 1642 after having spent his declining years imprisoned in his own study, unable to engage in scientific research, or to communicate with his intellectual peers. Darwin's Origin of Species was published in 1859 over two centuries later, and the "Monkey Trial" of John Scopes was held in 1925 in Dayton, Tennessee.

3 18. Those who responded #1, 2, 4, or 5 receive the prescription:

> Anselm based his chain of logic on the assumption that nothing greater than God can be conceived. In essence, his argument goes on to say this: If God were simply a figment of the imagination, some rainbow ideal dreamed up by people, it would be easy to conceive of something greater--namely, a force that truly existed outside the minds of people. But since nothing greater can be conceived, it follows that God does truly exist.

5 19. Those who responded #1, 2, 3, or 4 receive the prescription:

> The student objects to what technology has done to the human spirit. He objects to having become a number on the computer, and just another statistic. He is bewildered by the rapid acceleration in the rate of change, and generally appalled by the routine of contemporary life. He does not believe science has unlocked the door to undreamed of possibilities, but believes there are metaphysical truths still to be discovered.

n/a 20. Each response receives a prescription:

(1) If this were the question, it would mean that Bill is reevaluating the term "evil" itself. If his wife's death is simply a random accident, like all suffering, then perhaps no such thing as evil exists--at least, not in the traditional sense. The question "Why does God permit Evil?" would no longer be relevant.

(2) If this were the question, it would mean that Bill would

be withholding an evaluation of what happens to innocent people. To call their suffering "unfair" would be to imply that there is an ideal disposition of all events, and when has such a thing been promised? Bill would be coming to the conclusion that things happen as they will, not according to the human concepts of just and unjust. Such a conclusion, you will admit, is very painful for most people.

(3) If this were the question, Bill would be going all the way back to the Book of Job. The idea that he must have done something to deserve his suffering does occur to Job--reinforced by those who have come to comfort him. Many, however, would object to such a conclusion on the grounds that it fails to make a realistic assessment of what has happened to Bill--that in reality it represents an evasion of, not a coping with, the problem.

(4) If this were the question, it would mean that Bill was admitting the possibility that death is simply a part of life and comes randomly, not through a planned dispersal of justice. It is easier for many to believe that there is no plan behind life, than that the plan exists--and is sinister.

(5) If this were the question, many would applaud Bill's decision to open himself up to further growth, to accept what happens with stoic calm rather than to let his life grind to a halt. Some perhaps would feel he was dishonoring his wife's memory.

1 21. Those who responded #2, 3, 4, or 5 receive the prescription:

Zen Buddhism tends to communicate its teachings through cryptic parables like this one, often with a wary sense of humor. The "Wise One," or Zen master, usually answers an absurd question like "What is the truth?" in a startlingly abrupt way, which would probably mystify the questioner, but which nonetheless contains profound wisdom.

5 22. Those who responded #1, 2, 3, or 4 receive the prescription:

The whole reason for meditation in Buddhism is to achieve the wakeful state in which one is in direct contact with the moment as it really is. Those outside the Buddhist tradition often misunderstand meditation and suppose it to be a trance-like state of some sort.

1 23. Those who responded #2, 3, 4, or 5 receive the prescription:

Hindus believe the changing world of matter is an illusion (maya). Behind this world of appearance is an unchanging spirit, or world-soul, called Brahman. In Hinduism there is thus one soul, one absolute self, and all things are part of it. Buddhists do not believe in the existence of a self.

3 24. Those who responded #1, 2, 4, or 5 receive the prescription:

Buddhists do not believe in the existence of an absolute, separate self. In Buddhism the sense each of us has of being a personal entity--a "me" as opposed to "you"--is illusory. Through meditation one becomes detached from illusion. One comes to see his or her inner processes as simply mental phenomena, and views the processes of others in the same light. Consequently, one behaves toward oneself and others with equal objectivity and moral appropriateness, for in Buddhism no man is an island.

1 25. Those who responded #2, 3, 4, or 5 receive the prescription:

The aim of Buddhist meditation is to free oneself from the illusion of ego. As one meditates, one gradually finds that mind-chatter is beginning to disappear. Mind-chatter, of course, is the undirected flow of thoughts which engulfs the meditator "in the still and empty center." The narrator observes that in the beginning.

Answers

1 26. Those who responded #2, 3, 4, or 5 receive the prescription:

Westerners seek a "still center" rather than the "empty center" of the title. That is, they seek coherence (meaning inner integration and a sense of continuity) rather than simply "being," consciously aware of the present moment--detached from awareness of self, and able to exist discontinuously.

4 27. Those who responded #1, 2, 3, or 5 receive the prescription:

The young man in The Still and Empty Center, guided by the attitude of his family and society toward success and failure, feels that he cannot meditate "properly" and so cannot "succeed" at Buddhism. But success and failure are concepts that do not exist in the Buddhist outlook.

5 28. Those who responded #1, 2, 3, or 4 receive the prescription:

Voltaire published Candide in 1958. On one level, the novel is a satire on the eighteenth century philosophy of optimism, which held the view that disasters like the earthquake at Lisbon worked for an eventual, compensating good. Dr. Pangloss represents the philosopher Leibnitz, who popularized the belief that this is the best of all possible worlds and, therefore, that everything happens for the best.

5 29. Those who responded #1, 2, 3, or 4 receive the prescription:

The best possible answer is "all of the above." Western consciousness thinks of "self" as a territory that must be protected. In Western society, milestone achievements can be compared to territorial achievements, over which one presides as owner; and, of course, all of these values belong to a highly materialistic orientation to life.

MODULE VII

DRAMA: COMIC AND TRAGIC

TEACHING OVERVIEW

Like the art and music modules (II and III), Module VII can be taught in a technical sense. If drama is the instructor's personal discipline, or one which is quite important in his or her life, then the opportunity is there to offer the students at least a brief outline of high points in theatrical history: a Greek and Shakespearean tragedy, a comedy, and an illustration of what is happening in modern drama.

But the approach taken in both text and films is consistent with that of the course in general. It is fundamentally phycho-logical. Tragedy and comedy are the major forms of dramatic art, true; but they are also polar extremes of the psyche, contrasting dispositions of mind and heart--opposite ways of encountering and coping with what happens. In other words, the instructor without formal training in drama or dramatic criticism need not feel strange and insecure in these surroundings. A yin/yang principle is very much in evidence here, though now called by the names "comedy" and "tragedy."

The underlying premise is also familiar enough by now. The masks of comedy and tragedy can be worn by the same person. One must sustain a delicate balance between the tragic view that life will bring us all to our knees sooner or later, and the comic view that since things inevitably get so bad, all one can do is laugh. Somewhere between tears and laughter is a stable point which the humanist seeks as a refuge against both despair and derision.

CHECK LIST OF POINTS AND DISCUSSION TOPICS FROM TEXT

1. Basic differences between tragedy and comedy: feeling versus thought; free will versus determinism; the noble versus the mean (or less noble, or foolish) in human character.

2. Classical versus modern tragic heroes: high-born people of power, whose mistakes can devastate a whole society, versus common people who are not in control of their destiny (consequently can seldom devastate an entire society), but who are worth caring about because they are human beings.

3. Comic view of life rooted in common sense--in the normal, rational expectations of those who spend time in sober reflections. Since life continually violates those expectations, the refuge of the rational is laughter.

4. Sophoclean irony is a principle of dramatic structure whereby the audience knows the fate of the protagonist, but the latter does not.

   Euripidean irony is a particularly grim version of the tragic version of life. In this, things always turn out for the worst just when they look as if they're getting better. (Everyday life is full of Euripidean irony, isn't it? Or do we just notice it more than randomness?)

   Question: Does it help or hinder us to expect a Euripidean knife-twist whenever we plan something?

5. Hubris, the "perennial tragic flaw" of the tragic hero. Nixon as a contemporary possibility.

6. Single-mindedness -- the comic counterpart of hubris.

7. Charlie Chaplin's achievement: Merging tragic idealism and comic ineptitude--at times an almost miraculous synthesis.

8. Tragedy and comedy as resources for living.

    Tragedy: accepting life at its worst--allowing oneself to feel deeply, achieving catharsis.

    Comedy: facing life at its worst, but in sharp awareness of how this violates what ought to be; laughing to clear the air, without giving up one's rational expectations.

CHECK LIST OF POINTS AND DISCUSSION TOPICS FROM VIDEOTAPES

1. <u>The Tragic Vision</u>

    A. Tragedy arose when humanity became aware not only of death, but of the <u>unfairness of dying</u>.

    B. Greeks crystallized the tragic experience. They were the perfect people for it.

        1. Inherited the super gods of the Homeric age.

        2. Also developed a complete humanistic vision.

        3. This created a conflict: humanity as godlike, but frail, incomplete, almost but not quite there; mortal, not immortal like the gods; always doomed to inevitable failure.

    C. Oedipus as the archetypal tragic hero.

        1. Not tragic because he killed his father and married his mother.

        2. His is the tragedy of heroic pride--daring to insist upon his own version of reality; daring to demand the right to create his own destiny.

        3. Sophocles not "for" or "against" the gods. He recognizes their awesome power and knows human aspirations to godliness are pitiful.

    D. Hamlet is the archetypal tragedy about the loss of innocence.

1. Hamlet has believed in his mother's purity and the king's integrity.

2. Hamlet has believed in himself.

3. His world cracks apart, and he is almost buried in the ruins--but not quite! He is finally equal to the task; he confronts the king, and though the confrontation destroys him, Hamlet is able to rid the state of the king's evil.

4. _Hamlet_ is far more complex, though no less majestic, than _Oedipus_. The tragedy is more involved, however. The whole of reality is tragic in this play. Tragedy is the price one pays for maturity. Hamlet becomes a "mighty opposite" to Claudius, and learns to play the king's own game. Hamlet is perhaps corrupted, himself, in the transformation. (Look at what he does to Rosencrantz and Guildenstern.)

E. _King Lear_ is the archetypal tragedy of power.

1. Lear: In power too long--"executive privilege"--vulnerable to his daughters' plots in the complacency of his lofty position.

2. Storm on the heath a projection of the psychological storm created within Lear as illusions of his own greatness begin to crack. (Tie in with Hamlet in the matter of the loss of innocence. Lear's assumptions are a kind of innocence.)

3. The leveling of Lear: self-effacement and charity towards the "naked wretches" of the storm.

4. Euripidean irony of the moment in which the old King enters carrying the body of his daughter.

F. Why we need tragedy.

1. Suffering (as Lear demonstrates) brings out the best in us.

2. Humanity achieves monumentality in the act of tragically failing.

II. Knaves And Fools

A. Sense of humor - keen awareness of the incongruities of life (what happens though reason and common sense prefer otherwise).

B. Swiftian irony - pretending to approve of an act or attitude in order to heighten its irrationality.

C. Political cartoons of Wright raise interesting point: humor is not necessarily something we openly laugh at. Laughter can be an inward smile.

D. Distinction between the solemn and the serious. Solemn people generally lack humor--serious people don't.

TEACHING ALTERNATIVES

Text

1. Invite students to get together in groups outside of class and rehearse a scene from either a tragedy or a comedy to be performed or read before the others. Comedy generally works better than tragedy, because with untrained actors there is always the danger of having serious emotions ridiculed.

   But even so, this exercise gives the instructor a chance to apply some of the principles in the chapter to a specific example.

2. There are a number of excellent film versions of famous plays available for minimal rental fees. These could be assigned for viewing outside of class, with extra credit given for the writing of reviews. Students keeping a Journal could also view these films to good advantage.

   Electra, a Michael Cacoyannis production, with Irene Pappas. In Greek with English subtitles.

   Death of a Salesman, with Fredric March.

   Hamlet, with Laurence Olivier.

   A Streetcar Named Desire, with Marlon Brando and Vivien Leigh.

The Importance of Being Earnest, with Michael Redgrave and Edith Evans.

The Tragic Vision

Ask members of the class to listen to a television newscast and/or clip out newspaper accounts of recent events, with the idea of locating the tragic in real-life happenings. Some of these accounts can be read to or shared with the class, so that people can decide whether an event meets the requirements for tragedy or not.

Knaves And Fools

Ask members of the class to do some thinking about true, as opposed to superficial, humor. They may collect their thoughts in particular about people who seem to have humor and use it to defuse potentially solemn occasions; people who use comic lines at inappropriate times; people who seem to know just when a sad occasion has run its course and humor must now take over, etc. Make sure they are jotting down very specific examples (which can even be turned in for extra credit) so that they will have substantial material to share--not just vague and random ideas.

JOURNAL TOPICS

1. The text indicates that the story of Richard Nixon would probably provide ideal material for a modern tragedy, with all the heroic proportions of the great classics. Suppose you were going to write such a play. Briefly summarize the story, especially the ending in which the fate of the main character is revealed.

2. Do you know anyone who appears to be absolutely without a sense of humor? What is this person like? Why do you think he/she is without humor? In general, does he/she seem to be a happy person?

3. Do you know anyone who is overly oriented toward the tragic in life? Who seems to look on the melancholy side of everything? Why do you think this person is this way? What can you do to change things for the better?

4. Is the age and the society in which we live better suited for the writing of tragedies or comedies? State your reason.

5. Many people prefer neither pure tragedy, nor pure comedy, but a form of entertainment that is somewhere in between. Define what this entertainment is, and give some examples of it.

6. The text appears to disapprove of using laughter as a means of making fun of the unfortunate. But many people do laugh at minorities, the physically handicapped, the mentally slow. Why do you suppose they do?

MODULAR INTERIOR STRUCTURE

An effective way to communicate the distinction between the tragic and the comic is to first show the two videotapes, and then to take a particular theme or plot (such as the "Widow of Ephesus" story by Petronius) and demonstrate how it could be handled, both tragically and comically.

It is in the best interest of this module to keep both ends of the spectrum in full view throughout. One side should not be allowed to predominate, or the whole purpose of the unit will be lost.

ESSAY QUESTIONS

I. Text

1. Mention a modern personality who would make an ideal subject for a tragedy. Explain why.

2. Mention a personality you know who would make an ideal subject for a comedy. Explain why.

3. Think of a situation which could be viewed either tragically or comically. Describe it briefly in both senses.

4. Why are so many jokes about unfortunate people? Why are so many jokes about sex?

5. Is it better to laugh at everything that happens, or never to laugh at anything? Explain your answer.

6. The text says that we stop laughing when the banana peel becomes a true threat. Why?

II. The Tragic Vision

1. Most people would think that anyone who had done what Oedipus did must be very tragic indeed. But in Sophocles's play, Oedipus is tragic for a different reason. What is it?

2. Oedipus might have absolved himself of all blame by arguing that both the murder of the king and the incestuous marriage with the queen were predetermined by the gods. Instead, he takes full responsibility. Why do you think he did?

3. How may *King Lear* be regarded as a tragedy of executive privilege?

4. What profound truth about humanity does King Lear learn the hard way?

5. There is a scene in *King Lear* that illustrates Euripidean irony almost perfectly. What is that scene?

III. Knaves And Fools

1. What is the relationship of the title *Knaves And Fools* to the general subject of the film?

2. A banana peel is a classic ingredient of comedy--up to a point. What is that point?

3. Using Swift's "A Modest Proposal" as your example, explain briefly the nature and purpose of satire.

4. The narrator points out that "Mel Brooks is solemn, Woody Allen is serious." What distinction is he making?

5. Do you think we are living in a great age of comedy? One that needs, but does not have, great comedy? One that is better suited to tragedy?

6. Point out two or three characteristics of the Chaplin art that have caused critics to hail Charlie as the supreme comic genius of the films.

MODULE VIII

HOW THE MEDIUM AFFECTS THE MESSAGE

TEACHING OVERVIEW

The title of the module suggests a strong McLuhanesque bias, but in point of fact the text chapter deals with McLuhan only in the comparison drawn between print and visual media, while the videotapes offer the instructor a wide range of options.

One may, of course, elect to emphasize McLuhan's impact on media--particularly print. The text itself reflects the authors' desire to move away from the traditional print-heavy appearance of books. The pages are broken up by boxed inserts, illustrations, and an abundance of white space. The entire curriculum, with its strong video component, represents an attempt to utilize different media of instruction.

The big point of the unit, however, does not have to be McLuhan, but rather, the recognition of what a medium is, how it molds and limits what the message can be, and how one must not assume that any one medium can communicate or perceive all of reality. Perhaps the most novel feature of it is not the restatement of media information, but the fact that it deals with the senses as the media of perception. The film Intricate Eye treats blindness less as a disability than the substitution of one dominant medium for another. Some instructors may want to utilize this module to encourage their students to think about and actually engage in a variety of sense experiences.

CHECK LIST OF POINTS OR DISCUSSION TOPICS FROM TEXT

1. What is a medium? How does it make certain messages possible, and not others? Do we always read the message properly? (For example, "We'll call you when there's an opening.")

2. Coming of print--democratization of the word. The growth of print mystique. Isn't language in print somehow more authoritative than handwritten language?

3. McLuhan and the raising of our consciousness about media. Side effect (perhaps not intended by McLuhan at all)--a mad scramble to substitute for print medium. The multimedia forces.

   Note: In the confusion, "media" can now mean only television, or it can mean multimedia. If we're going to make good use of McLuhan, let us be nonjudgmental about the term "media," and try to discern what it is that each medium does best.

4. Instead of attempting to cover the entire range of mass media and their effect on us, the text focuses on the "late, late show," and offers a few examples of how values were instilled into many of us by the silver screen. One is the film "Gone With The Wind," which concluded with the heroine's realization that there's no place like home, and gave Depression-weary audiences the satisfaction of leaving Scarlett with a roof over her head.

5. Some of the effects of television: rapid growing up; the need for continual entertainment; the sense that we have control over time and space; an impatience with the untelevised.

6. The day of the computer is upon us, and right now there is a fierce debate going on between advocates of high tech and many humanists who fear that the precision of the computer could make people mentally lazy and less curious about the unknown.

7. Other media under discussion include video games (giving the illusion of human control over cosmic events); the telephone (discouraging an expanded use of language); clothes (in what sense are we what we wear?); body language (the subtext behind what we say, and often not even noticed).

8. Architecture as a medium. The buildings we create have a statement to make. Contrast the Empire State Building with its narrowing spires, proudly announcing an old-fashioned hierarchy, and the World Trade Center with its promise of democratic glass through which we can, however, see nothing.

CHECK LIST OF POINTS OR DISCUSSION TOPICS FROM VIDEOTAPES

I. The Intricate Eye

A. The assumption made by sighted people that reality is a visual phenomenon, and that without sight no one can fully perceive what really is.

B. The indications in the environment around us that the sense of sight is mandatory (as is having full use of one's limbs).

C. Color exists for blind English teacher only as an abstraction--words. But by the same token, no one can be sure that anyone else sees the same colors. Even the sighted are imprisoned within the limitations of the medium.

II. Television, The Electric Art

A. Re: opening montage of mass media effects. How much of what we "know" is "known" because of the media?

B. According to Tay Voye, TV programmers use ratings as their guide to programming. But which comes first? An imaginative programmer who creates the ratings--or the taste of the viewing public?

C. The Zamora trial. Defendant found guilty, so line of defense didn't work. Does this say the last word on the impact of TV violence?

D. Agnew's famous speech about "media" is now ironic, since the mass media were partially responsible for his own demise.

Does this close the issue? Do mass media have extraordinary, even unfair powers, nonetheless?

E. If TV were suddenly to vanish . . .

TEACHING ALTERNATIVES

Text

1. Tell class to disperse and take walks, individually or in small groups, around the campus, jotting down every sample of campus media they can find--stairs, ramps (or lack of them), elevators (open to public, or available only to keyholders), etc. Then have a sharing session about what such "media analysis" has disclosed.

2. Divide the class into small groups, each of which is charged with the task of redesigning the campus in such a way as to make it "say" that the student is all-important here. One person in each group can transfer the design to newsprint. After time is called, have all the newsprint taped to the walls for sharing.

3. To dramatize the important point that the medium _is_ the message, select a particular message and then invite various members of the class, singly or in groups, to deliver it via different media. Take, for example, the message "John is in love with Mary," and present it as a:

   formal letter from a college counselor
   personal letter from Mary to John
   personal letter from John to Mary
   Sunday sermon
   political speech

The Intricate Eye

An extremely effective exercise for developing empathy with the unsighted is to pair the students off, having one person keep his or her eyes shut tightly while the other leads him or her around the campus. After a set amount of time, the two may exchange roles.

Television, The Electric Art

1. Divide into groups, charging each with the conception, design, and then the performance of a television commercial which powerfully persuades the viewer to pay an exorbitant amount for a product which serves no practical or esthetic function whatever.

2. Have each group design and present a commercial which takes only 60 seconds. The aim is to be as professional, all-inclusive, and artistic as possible. This exercise helps to make the students more aware of what not only a commercial, but any communication is trying to do, and to encourage them to evaluate in terms of purpose and degree of success relative to that purpose.

JOURNAL TOPICS

1. On your way to school, or the next time you have occasion to go into town, make a mental note of all the evidences of both closed and open environments. Describe some of these. In general, is the surrounding area a closed or open environment?

2. Take any idea and--instead of writing about it line by line--experiment with a non-linear approach. Combine words, pictures, diagrams, and other alternatives to linearity.

3. Project the Top Five television shows for next season. You can play it straight, or have a little fun here. Give a summary of each one as it might be found in the TV Guide.

4. The text includes clothing styles as a medium, since most people seem to dress in some characteristic fashion that communicates some sort of message. Describe your own way of dressing. What statement do you think you are making?

5. The course you are taking is modular in nature. A module is a medium, as is a series of modules comprising a whole course. Describe modular communication as a means of educational communication. Contrast this with some other means.

6. If you were suddenly to become blind, how would you adjust? Would it be easy, or difficult for you?

MODULAR INTERIOR STRUCTURE

The Intricate Eye is concerned with media of perception, while The Electric Art has to do with a major medium of communication. One can say that the first film takes an overview of media, while the second describes a specific example. Or, one cay say that the first film shows what media are, while the second describes how a specific medium can be used. The text chapter can be pointed in any of the above directions.

Another very distinct possibility is to talk about the emergence of visual media, along with the diminishing role of print, and then use The Intricate Eye as an illustration of how important the visual has become in our society; how the unsighted often must contend with the assumption that there is no genuine substitute for the visual; and how the unsighted can assert their own media, regardless.

ESSAY QUESTIONS

I. Text

1. Give three examples of media and messages through which one may convey feelings of love and devotion other than words. (Remember, each example must be from a distinct medium.)

2. McLuhan pointed out how the invention of print turned people "linear" in their orientation. What exactly does this mean?

3. In popular rock music, words do not seem to be used the way words are in poetry--or even in slow love songs. What is the point of having words that few, if any, can hear?

4. The text analyzes some effects of old movies in their time. Discuss a recent film that you think is having a particular effect on audiences.

5. Which of your surroundings communicates most directly what you are like as a person. Describe them.

6. What is body language? In what sense is it a medium?

II. The Intricate Eye

1. The word "handicapped" is widely used in our society. Has the concept of media made any difference in your understanding of "handicapped"?

2. McLuhan said the medium is the message. What did he mean?

3. Color for the English teacher in the program is not a medium, but a . . . what? Explain.

III. The Electric Art

1. The debate continues over whether television is an art form, or not. Discuss one element that would justify calling it an art, and one element that would not.

2. The defendant was found guilty in the Zamora trial. Do you think the verdict proves that television does not have an adverse effect on young minds?

3. Should the television industry be nationalized to ensure that it does not adversely condition the feelings and thoughts of us all?

4. Complete this statement: "Right now, the top TV show is _____________________ because . . ."

SURVEY 4 PRESCRIPTIONS

Answers

5 1. Those who responded #1, 2, 3, or 4 receive the prescription:

Since any of the first four options offers a valid explanation of what McLuhan means by "The medium is the message," your answer is all right, but is not the best answer you could have chosen. If you reread the question stem carefully, you will see that by selecting your option, you have excluded the others, whereas the option "Any of the above" is all-inclusive and is therefore what you should have chosen.

3 2. Those who responded #1, 2, 4, or 5 receive the prescription:

All of the options except number three, "A tree falling in the forest with no one to hear it," represent vehicles by which messages are either sent or received. By contrast, a tree is neither vehicle nor message, but concrete reality. The fact that no one is around to hear it fall reinforces the idea that there are no media involved.

1 3. Those who responded #2, 3, 4, or 5 receive the prescription:

While many involved in educational television keep hoping that the result will be a "medium transfer," by which students will become so intrigued by the video presentation of an idea that they will want to read more about it, research has yet to show a definite correlation between television and the desire to read more widely.

3 4. Each incorrect response receives a prescription:

(1) For some people this may be true, but I for one would rather read a book than listen to most speeches. In any event, the statement has no relevance to the influence of print on awareness.

Answers

(2) I have no statistics right at hand, but I would bet this statement is true. It is not, however, the right answer since it has no relevance to the influence of print on awareness. Ponder your options more carefully.

(4) This is the kind of statement that sounds reasonable, but how could one ever go about proving it? And what would be the point? It has no relevance to the influence of print on awareness. Ponder your options more carefully.

(5) Reread the question, then look at the first four options. You will see that only option three makes a statement about the print medium and awareness.

1 5. Those who responded #2, 3, 4, or 5 receive the prescription:

The so-called "McLuhanites" of the 1960's (not necessarily speaking for McLuhan himself) frequently burst into print to object to people who burst into print, and generally carried on tirades against print-oriented people, who they said were victims of a very narrow view of the world. In other words, people who read all the time were supposedly incapable of seeing reality as a whole.

2 6. Each incorrect response receives a prescription:

(1) Many persons would agree with your answer. Certainly the defense for Ronny Zamora was that he suffered from television addiction. However, the jury who found the boy guilty either disagreed with the statement, or considered it quite irrelevant to the case.

(3) This option would make Marshall McLuhan very happy. He would agree completely with the sentiment in it. However, one cannot imagine that a jury would be deliberating abstractions. The verdict clearly suggests that in the jury's eyes, the television medium was not directly responsible for a murder.

(4) Many believe this statement completely, especially politicians, who often blame newscasters for ruining their image with the public. But the statement also has no relevance to the question, which you must not have read very carefully. Or perhaps you were not able to view "Television, The Electric Art," which contains an account of the Zamora trial.

(5) In a sense, the television medium was indeed on trial along with Ronny Zamora, for if the boy had been found not guilty, the verdict could have led to sweeping changes in the kinds of programs aired. But as stated, this option does not relate logically to the question stem. Had the option read "The television medium was considered not to be responsible for inciting young viewers to violence," it would have been a reasonable answer to the question. If you reread the options, you will see that number two does say just that.

1 7. Those who responded #2, 3, 4, or 5 receive the prescription:

Options two through five do hint at controversy, but you must realize that "controversial" does not always relate to drastic or radical ideas. McLuhan's inventory of media and their effects set a lot of people talking about a subject, media, which was quite novel to many of them. Some took exception to what they considered to be McLuhan's dogmatic assertions about matters like the psychological differences between print oriented and visually oriented people.

1 8. Those who responded #2, 3, or 5 receive the prescription:

Newscasters and program directors interviewed admitted that sensationalism was frequently the basis for a choice among possible news stories. They agreed that the public was less interested in facts for their own sake than in excitement. Remember the old cliche that a dog's biting a man is not news, but the opposite definitely is. Perhaps someone will soon make a study of why people seem to enjoy alarming news--news that says disaster of some sort is on the way.

Those who responded #4 receive the prescription:

> Your answer deserves special mention. Those interviewed for this program definitely indicated that the selection of material for television news programming often depends upon sensationalism. At the same time, one suspects that the moral viewpoint of the newscaster must sometimes enter into the selection process. It would be difficult to imagine a newscaster's remaining unbiased after years in the business.

4 9. Those who responded #1, 2, 3, or 5 receive the prescription:

> "Gilgamesh," named for its tragic hero, is the oldest known work of literature, discovered on tablets of baked clay which had been buried for at least five thousand years in the ruins of Mesopotamia.

1 10. Those who responded #2, 3, 4, or 5 receive the prescription:

> Arthur Miller is of major importance in modern drama, not only for Death of a Salesman, but for his articulate plea on behalf of common-man tragedy. In an article written shortly after the first production of "Salesman," Miller said that tragedy had been influenced for too long by Aristotle's observation that the tragic hero is necessarily highborn. It seems probable that Miller was being deliberately non-Aristotelian in the very title of his play.

4 11. Those who responded #1, 2, 3, or 5 receive the prescription:

> As you know, the dividing line between the comic and the tragic is often very thin indeed. The films of Chaplin illustrate this point quite well. What generally keeps a comedy from ever becoming profoundly tragic is the fact that the comic hero is usually unaware of his follies or the dangers which surround him--or at least he does not suffer because of them. In contrast, the tragic hero is hypersensitive to his plight and to the pain he is experiencing.

Answers

5 12. Each incorrect response receives a prescription:

(1) It is true that emotion is intensified as one views a tragedy, but the end result of the experience, according to Aristotle, was the purgation of emotion. Aristotle, a supreme rationalist, would never have approved of an art form which left the audience in an emotional state.

(2) It is true that emotion is actualized by a profoundly stirring experience, but for Aristotle the end result of the experience has the purgation of emotion. A supreme rationalist, Aristotle would never have approved of an art form which left the audience in a state of "actualized" emotion.

(3) In a way, one could talk about a tragedy's leaving us with the "opposite" of the emotions aroused in us by the events on the stage. But one must understand by this not opposite emotions, but an opposite--that is, non-emotional--condition. Therefore, the best answer in this case is "purgation," which is the rational state attained after emotion has run its course.

(4) As a supreme rationalist, Aristotle would have been perplexed by the suggestion that tragedy ought to reinforce emotion. In contrast, he believed the point of tragedy has to arouse emotions in order to purge the viewer of them--leaving him in a calm, rational state--better able to cope with life's experiences.

5 13. Each incorrect response receives a prescription:

(1) While this chapter points out that a sense of humor is basic to the rational and moral foundation of society, it does not equate humor with frivolousness. Quite the contrary--it is the fundamental seriousness of humor that is stressed here.

(2) The killer instinct was related to the viewing of tragedy in the sense that, according to one theory at least, audiences of a tragedy sometimes take

perverse pleasure in enjoying the suffering of the characters, but the end result is a beneficial purgation of such destructive feelings.

(3) If a comic character has a tragic flaw, then by definition he or she becomes a tragic character. A comedy remains a comedy precisely because the hero is either blind to his plan, or does not suffer because of it. It is hard to laugh while we are feeling the tragic pain of another human being.

(4) The chapter clearly avoids taking sides. It does say that a sense of humor is basic to the rational and moral foundation of society, but it does not suggest that either comedy or tragedy is more appropriate for human beings than the other.

3 14. Those who responded #1, 2, 4, or 5 receive the prescription:

Euripides loved to end some of his plays with a cruel twist of fate. The possibility of a happy ending is raised, and then it is plucked away from the audience--thus intensifying the pain. A convicted murderer in a Euripidean tragedy would no doubt be executed because something happened to retard the arrival of the stay, which finally comes--too late.

4 15. Those who responded #1, 2, 3, or 5 receive the prescription:

Hirsch put Charlie Chaplin at the top of the list primarily because of his "Little Tramp" character, an endearing figure toward whom audiences felt warm human sympathies, while at the same time laughing at both the knavery and foolishness of the character. Besides, the Little Tramp always emerged optimistic and resilient, never crushed by life or the big city towering above him.

2 16. Those who responded #1 receive the prescription:

Shakespeare not only could have created the final act of "Lear," but he actually did so. You may have selected this option because you hastily paired off author and play in your mind, without reading the question stem carefully. Euripides, with his love of cruel and ironic twists, could have devised the ending of "Lear."

Those who responded #3, 4, or 5 receive the prescription:

Shakespeare, not Euripides, wrote King Lear, but the final act greatly resembles the cruel endings of some of the Greek tragedian's works. During the 18th century the last act of "Lear" was considered so barbarically cruel that the play was almost never performed anywhere.

1 17. Those who responded #2, 3, 4, or 5 receive the prescription:

Tragedy arouses and intensifies emotion as the viewer watches the grim proceedings building to a devastating climax, while comedy causes us to laugh by presenting events that violate our rational expectations of life. The end result of either a tragic or a comic experience in the theater is that we reclaim our psychological equilibrium. We are shocked into it, so to speak. There is just so much we can feel, or just so much we can laugh at. Out of the renewed tranquility comes clarity of thought.

4 18. Those who responded #1, 2, 3, or 5 receive the prescription:

If you answered "disabled," "handicapped," "unfortunate," or "well adjusted under the circumstances," you were projecting your own value system into the program. The English teacher who was the subject of the film knows herself to be working in alternate media. The other terms are used by sighted persons to describe those without sight--seldom, if ever, by the unsighted themselves.

5 19. Those who responded #1, 2, 3, or 4 receive the prescription:

Ms. Howard's remarks at the very conclusion of the

Answers

film indicate that if she were somehow to develop the sense of sight, she would be confused, disoriented, and have a hard time adjusting to new kinds of reality which do not now exist for her. We must remember that she has never been sighted, and has no consciousness of "missing" something.

2 20. Those who responded #1, 3, 4, or 5 receive the prescription:

As the text states, the purpose of "the power of the medium" chapter was to alert the reader to the many ways in which messages can be conveyed. By becoming aware of the way different media affect our consciousness, we can learn both to recognize and resist the "sub-texts" of mass media and to be more sophisticated audiences.

2 21. Those who responded #1, 3, 4, or 5 receive the prescription:

The invention of the printing press caused a revolution in the way people received information. Ideas that had formerly been available only to priests and scholars in expensive manuscripts now were available to the general public. Anyone who could read could now read independently and form judgments without relying on the views of authorities. It was the beginning of a democratic process.

1 22. Those who responded #2, 3, 4, or 5 receive the prescription:

Ball parks sometimes, but not always, exclude those who do not or cannot pay an admission fee. Some, but by no means all, beaches do the same. Both streets and shopping malls can exclude some access on occasion. But a public school is generally organized and designed in such a way as to control the movements of students by restrictive rules.

2 23. Those who responded #1, 3, 4, or 5 receive the prescription:

The effective television commercial was described in

terms that might easily apply to a well-written short story. Both are highly condensed art forms; situations and characters are established quickly, developed, and brought to a swift conclusion that has the desired impact on the audience.

3 24. Those who responded #1, 2, 4, or 5 receive the prescription:

Oedipus is described as a man who stubbornly denies reality. In rejecting the truth that the blind prophet Teiresias tells about the King's past deeds, and in refusing to connect the old shepherd's story to the original prophecy (when the entire audience is doing just that), Oedipus brings about his tragic downfall.

5 25. Those who responded #1, 2, 3, or 4 receive the prescription:

The text chapter states that comedies like M*A*S*H always have a norm of common sense against which the comic elements are measured. In M*A*S*H, Hawkeye is the rational norm against which the irrational singlemindedness of the comic characters appears ridiculous.

1 26. Those who responded #2, 3, 4, or 5 receive the prescription:

The text makes the point that the great tragedies emphasize free choice. In fact, the tragic hero attains grandeur to some extent because he has himself made the choice that leads to his destruction. In many modern tragedies, however, the protagonist may be the helpless victim of forces beyond his control--social institutions, an inhuman environment, or even his genetic makeup. In this case, some critics say, he is merely pathetic--not tragic.

2 27. Those who responded #1, 3, 4, or 5 receive the prescription:

"The Intricate Eye" makes the point that in the

Answers

modern electronic world, people depend to a great extent on the sense of sight for perceiving things. However, perception is an "intricate" process in which all the senses convey information. For example, the blind teacher, through the sense of touch, is able to read braille and to experience texture and shape esthetically.

5 28. Those who responded #1, 2, 3, or 4 receive the prescription:

Most modern glass buildings are so constructed that the viewer cannot discern where the true power resides, or what is indeed going on inside. But glass allows those within to have a clear view of the outside. Business needs to observe without being observed.

3 29. Those who responded #1, 2, 4, or 5 receive the prescription:

If you will recall, the narrator of "A Modest Proposal" is supposedly a member of the English gentry, who accepts quite calmly the wretched state of the Irish poor and suggests a "rational" way to alleviate the horrible condition--namely, by slaughtering the children of the poor and serving them as food for the English wealthy. Since Swift, innumerable writers have imitated the comic irony of this piece by pretending to endorse a point of view which they really despise, and to exaggerate it to such a degree that the reader is convinced that it is appalling.

MODULE IX

THEMES IN THE HUMANITIES: MYTH

TEACHING OVERVIEW

Like art or music, mythology represents a vast discipline--enough material for several courses, let alone one week! Once again, the instructor must make some pertinent choices and select those focal points which can be most successfully handled in the time allotted. A possible premise for the module is that we learn more about ourselves from the mythology that helps us steer our lives. Another is that we learn more about our culture from understanding the mythology that has helped to shape it. Still another is that there are different kinds of myths--from myth as pre-scientific explanation to myth as insight.

In both text and films one will find Jung's theory that myths are expressions of the racial memory, the collective unconscious, repositories of the great archetypes without which there would be no human civilization as we know it. One will also find Joseph Campbell's presentation of myth as that which shapes both the individual and society. ("Myths are public dreams; dreams are private myths.")

There are so many good reasons for acquiring some background in myth that the instructor may wish to stress the major myth plots and characters that are summarized in the chapter and briefly touch upon their enduring significance. The world myth (monomyth) is dealt with in a fairly detailed manner and could easily be the focal point of the module.

There is abundant material, however, for the instructor who enjoys teaching mythology as literature, pointing out some common themes, symbols, and characterizations, without getting into archetypes or racial memory or cultural significance.

Regardless of the approach taken, the student should come away from this module relieved of the misconception that myths are fallacies, made-up versions of reality, appropriate for primitive people but hardly for the enlightened society of today. To overlook scientific or space mythology is to perpetuate the misunderstanding; and to ignore Star Wars on the grounds that it does not constitute a real contribution to the humanities is to perpetuate an elitist attitude.

CHECK LIST OF POINTS OR DISCUSSION TOPICS FROM TEXT

1. Two contrary definitions of myth are "truth" and "untruth," but myth can also stand somewhere between these poles.

2. Myth can be the way primitive people explained things they did not understand. But it can also be the way humankind has always made the vast universe accessible to its understanding.

3. For Jung, myth is the collective unconscious, the racial memory, a vast repository of archetypes of models (such as the hero) by which human beings make sense out of experience.

4. Much Greek mythology probes the darkest corners of psychological humanity and can be said to be a starting place for a study of human behavior.

5. Greek mythology is especially obsessed with the family theme--what family relationships do to us.

6. The monomyth, hero myth, or world myth is the universal myth plot that seems to tell the whole human story. Use Oedipus or Theseus to summarize the monomyth--unusual birth, exile, rise to greatness, fall from greatness, second exile, mysterious death.

7. Myth themes and symbols--magic, words, numbers, broken commands, circles, and journeys.

8. If space is a new mythic frontier, we also have remnants of myth as explanation, representing what is not always the noblest expression of mythology. Examples: Nazism and the myth of white supremacy.

CHECK LIST OF POINTS OR DISCUSSION TOPICS FROM VIDEOTAPES

I. Myths: The Collective Dreams of Mankind

A. Opening of film is a dramatization of a ritual involving the mandala symbol. The mandala as an omnipresent symbol of unity--the unity of phenomena and that of the psychic life.

The significance of the mandala is not how phenomena are interpreted, but rather *that* they are interpreted at all--that from earliest times human beings seemed to require a symbolic figure that would represent an interpretive principle. The roundness of the mandala tells us that humanity wanted the whole enterprise to make perfect sense.

B. The voyage and the quest as universal mythic structures.

This is a good place to bring in *Star Wars* or, if students can still view it, Kubrick's *2001*, as an example of contemporary views of the quest.

C. Arthurian legend: a vision of an ideal government.

Are we waiting for a contemporary Arthur to pull a new Excalibur from a stone? (e.g., Ted Kennedy, Ralph Nader, Gary Hart)

D. Eden myths: The Aryan "pure" society; the classless society; the New World.

One might add the commune myths of the 1960's. Do we have any new Eden myths? (Health spas? Jogging camps?)

E. Space mythology: flying saucers; "interplanetary saviors" (as in Close Encounters of the Third Kind); apocalypse (imminent destruction of the planet); explorations of Mars and other planets ("new breeding grounds for life").

II. The Dream Of The Hero

A. Source of myths in the unconscious mind of the individual and in the collective unconscious of the race.

B. The hero as the indispensable mythic projection.

(1) We need heroes to believe in, and we need to believe in ourselves as heroes, central figures, power figures.

(2) Characteristics of the hero. (See Marshall Fishwick's analysis of John F. Kennedy as the prototypal hero in Study Guide Module V.)

C. How the story of Theseus embodies the monomyth.

D. Significance of the monomyth.

(1) Why the inevitable fall of the hero?

(2) Why do people reject the hero?

(3) Why is the hero's greatness recognized only after his death? (Or is his death the indispensable grounds by which he is judged great?)

(4) Is there a vicious circle here? Do people create, then destroy their own heroes?

Text

1. Divide the class into small groups.

   Task: Locate and summarize a contemporary myth which serves as an explanation for a phenomenon. Each group should then share with the rest of the class its myth, the premise behind it, and a list of reasons for the popularity of the myth. The explanation should be an analysis of the psychological need which the believers have for the myth.

2. In small groups, share with each other some of the influential fairy tales in your formative years, and what you now (looking back) think they did for (or to) you. Have a spokesperson for each group jot down the data, and then present a general summary before the entire community. Remember, a fairy tale is defined in the text as a myth that does not tell the whole story.

3. Since humanity is always in need of new myths, why not use this module as an opportunity to have the class produce some?

   Individually--and then shared with others.
   By groups--and then acted out before the class.
   As a class ensemble exercise--beginning as an improvisation on an agreed upon situation or set of characters--and see what happens.

4. Divide into small groups. Give each group a different set of mythic elements. For example:

   a magic phrase and a curse;
   a journey and a mandala;
   a curse and a quest;
   a sword (or gun, or laser gun) and a magic phrase.

   The group must weave a myth story out of the elements it is given, and then narrate the story--either together, or using one spokesperson--to the entire community.

Myths: The Collective Dreams Of Mankind

1. Have students bring to class magazine ads, newspaper stories, etc., in which they have discovered components of modern mythology. TV commercials, jotted down, also work well. Remember the Ajax White Knight? Mr. Clean? Colonel Sanders?

2. Divide into groups.

   Task: Discuss and determine which collective dreams are emerging from our present-day society. What are our hopes and fears? That someone will invent a car that runs on water? That we are coming to the end of our freewheeling life-style, and face an uncertain but undoubtedly very different future? That we may have to confront the possibility that the human race will not survive? That someone will come along and show us how to make a new beginning? Who? What sort of person?

The Dream Of The Hero

Divide into small groups. Using Fishwick's presentation of Kennedy as the prototype of the hero (in Study Guide), take the elements of the hero story and see how many apply to current figures. The idea, of course, is not that newsworthy people accidentally seem to fall into this pattern, but that *we* somehow find the people who do, and make them newsworthy because WE NEED THE PATTERN.

JOURNAL TOPICS

1. Write a short autobiography in mythic terms. Describe your birth, your mission in life, the villains you must outwit, your magic powers, and your eventual recognition as a great being.

2. Describe two fairy tales that had a tremendous impact on you as you were growing up. Why did they?

3. Describe two fairy tales you would definitely read to your children. Indicate what importance you think they would have.

4. Indicate two Greek myths which in your opinion offer valid insights into human behavior. Why?

5. Why do most myths seem to be tragic? Why are some of our major myth figures also tragic personalities (e.g., Gandhi, Kennedy, King)?

6. Jung argued that, since the mandala has been an important symbol for many different cultures, its circular shape must relate to humankind's way of ordering things. Why circular? Why not some other shape?

7. Magic words and phrases play a very prominent role in myths. Why this eternal fascination with the mystic properties of language?

8. The creation of myths never seems to stop, no matter how much scientific knowledge humanity attains. Other than space myths, describe two or three current myths relating to science itself.

MODULAR INTERIOR STRUCTURE

As in the preceding module, the two films have a general/particular relationship. The Collective Dreams is a broad introduction to mythology from a psychological and anthropological point of view. The Dream of the Hero focuses on the monomyth and its significance.

A workable procedure is to divide the week into the following: 25% for discussion of myth as an explanation both for the ancients and for us. 75% for a treatment of mythology as a cumulative tradition of insights and a way of making sense of experience. Or ancient and modern myths can be handled in parallel fashion. Some possibilities are:

> the journey: Theseus/astronauts
> the quest: Theseus and the minotaur/saving the princess in Star Wars
> the hero: Theseus/Kennedy, or King.

ESSAY QUESTIONS

I. Text

1. Explain briefly the mythology underlying each of the following statements:

   a. "The honeymoon is over."
   b. "Knock on wood."
   c. "I'm right back where I started."

2. Many myths and fairy tales are fundamentally sexist in nature. Discuss any two examples.

3. Discuss any two archetypes you can identify in your own early development. Did they help or hinder that development?

4. Why do you think there is a world myth? What might it tell us about ourselves?

5. Is the purpose of myths to make life bearable or comprehensible?

II. Myths: The Collective Dreams Of Mankind

1. What does the phrase "collective dreams" mean to you?

2. Why do you suppose that from earliest times myth-makers represented life as a journey? What is this saying?

3. Carl Jung views myths as collections of universal archetypes. What does he mean?

4. Are myths always beneficial to people? Can you think of one example of how a myth proved disastrous?

5. Summarize in your own words what the film says about the mythology of space. What do space myths mean to us at this point in our history?

III. The Dream Of The Hero

1. Commentators of the current scene often indicate that

young people today need heroes and there are none to be found. First, why do young people need heroes? Second, is there a lack of heroes today? Third, why or why not?

2. What significance do you find in the fact that many myth heroes suffer a rejection from the people and often die in obscurity?

3. The central character of a movie is usually called "the hero." From your viewing of recent films, would you say that the main characters are heroes in the mythological sense? Explain your answer.

MODULE X

THEMES IN THE HUMANITIES: LOVE

TEACHING OVERVIEW

Though no modules up to this point have been dealt with relative to each other, we come now to a real possibility of doing so. Love and the two themes which follow--happiness and death--can be shown to have something in common as themes in the humanities.

1. Each is enormously important to great numbers of people.
2. Each can be found in literature, art, and philosophy for many centuries.
3. Each defies a universal, absolute definition, but can be shown to be relative to time, place, and culture.

In this module we also have a chronological approach, tracing the concept of love from its first (apparent) appearance in Greek literature and thought to some present-day dilemmas surrounding the much used, and little understood, term. Instructors who have been longing for a chance to treat a theme historically will find a golden opportunity here.

However, a categorical approach is also possible--e.g., love of family; friendship (in all its guises); loyalties; intimacy; altruism; and self-love. Each category can be shown to be relevant, at least sometimes, to the elusive definition of love. Each poses its problems for us--and a humanities course can offer much insight into the problems.

The first videotape, Love: Myth and Mystery, warns the student that no one has ever located an absolute definition. The second, Roles We Play, shows the confusions in which people live as a consequence of sex-role stereotyping, based upon narrow definitions of what love is and how it should operate in our society.

CHECK LIST OF POINTS OR DISCUSSION TOPICS FROM TEXT

1. The chapter is about love in all its guises and disguises. It is about love as historical phenomenon, as compromise, and as art.

2. Family love is where it all starts and, for many, where the phenomenon becomes hopelessly opaque to the understanding. Family love is often difficult because of the tension between sense of obligation and the modern emphasis on liberation. A family has to be made to "work," and each member of it needs to be sensitive to the problems of the others.

3. Friendship can be the strongest form of love, provided we know that friends can be freely chosen and we know why we have chosen them.

4. Platonic love--mistakenly thought by some to be a relationship without physical gratification. In actuality, Platonic love involves primarily an emotional and intellectual oneness. It is the adoration of beauty in another's mind, rather than solely the body, although physical relationship is not an impossibility in Platonic love.

5. Altruism--ideal vs. reality. Our culture has been strongly influenced by the Christian concept of loving another more than oneself. The question remains: How much self-interest underlies altruistic behavior?

6. Self-love --not the same as self-centered love. Self-love is a realistic appraisal of one's assets and liabilities, with no misplaced sense of unworth.

7. Two pervasive models of human relationships, which are found widely in the arts, are romantic love and Victorian love. Romantic love has its origins in Medieval tales of gallantry, of dashing knights and their fair ladies, and of serenades under balconies. It has perpetuated, and continues to do so, the myth of "the right someone" for each of us--decreed by heaven. Victorian love is more or less the basis of still surviving concepts of appropriate male and female sex roles, despite the many forward strides of human rights movements.

   Question: Is the difficulty experienced by supporters of ERA in persuading people to support the amendment indicative of Victorian attitudes?

CHECK LIST OF POINTS OR DISCUSSION TOPICS FROM VIDEOTAPES

I. Love: Myth and Mystery

   A. Story of Eloise and Abelard illustrates the Greek and Christian separation of physical and spiritual love, and the conflicts--even tragedy--it caused. Legend suggests that both kinds of love could be, and were, present in one relationship, though the institutions of medieval society required the dichotomy and the choice.

   B. The narrator:

      1. Why is he writing a book about love with that title?

      2. Is he basically cynical or romantic about love?

      3. Is he modern or old-fashioned in his attitude or his problem?

   C. Interesting to note that the definitions of love surveyed by the narrator more or less cancel each other out. From the beginning, then, the idea that love was the noblest of human experiences has been challenged.

   D. The film doesn't include this, but the Ik tribe in a remote mountainous area of Africa does not have a word for love or for related states, such as charity and sharing. Does this suggest that love is strictly cultural in nature?

E. In the Bible, one can observe the steady development of the concept of universal love and the identification of this with God.

   Note: Some observers have labeled the Judeo-Christian idea of love the most powerful single idea ever advanced.

F. The impact of St. Paul. The soul is greater than the body. Sexual love, except in marriage, is sinful--an animalistic trait which humanity must transcend.

G. Medieval romance and courtly love tradition (from which the romantic ideal derives). Courtly love was a codified relationship between persons unmarried (at least to each other) in which the woman was venerated, put on a pedestal, and adored by the lovesick man, who had to deny his base desires and substitute poetry and serenades. This code of gallantry (chivalry) is still with us, at least as an ideal; and when many girls dream of "Mr. Right," he is often wearing medieval armor.

H. Freud's impact on the romantic ideal of love.

I. Fromm: Most of the time we seek "love" not for its own sake, but as a means of ending a state of separateness. Human beings, says Fromm, cannot bear to be alone.

II. Roles We Play

A. Opening narration is not intended as absolute historical fact, but as an interpretation of history in terms of sexual inequality. (The burden of proof, however, would seem to be on the side of those who would attest otherwise!)

B. The significance of A Doll's House, 1879, the first major play about liberation from a socially-manufactured sex role.

C. The concept of a sex role (of any kind of role) needs clarification and warrants discussion.

Note: The course design team shares the view that a role is not necessarily a masquerade, but is a characteristic disposition toward a certain kind of event which a person adopts, either voluntarily or because of conditioning. Hence, one individual is comprised of a great many "roles," but surely not all of them can be voluntary, or feel really comfortable.

D. Questions about the two-and-a-half couples on whom the film centers:

1. Is David macho? Is Nora a closet housewife?

2. Is Claire a doormat, as Nora insists she is?

3. Are David and Tom in competition with each other? Is it okay if they are?

4. Why did Dennis marry Gail? Or Gail, Dennis?

5. Does Gail play the perennial cheerleader role for her own sake?

E. The film does not try to solve the complex problems of sex role-playing, but it does convey the thought that people need to know what roles they are playing, and why--and that they need to be comfortable in their roles.

TEACHING ALTERNATIVES

Roles We Play

1. An effective exercise is to divide the class between men and women. Each side of the room is asked to discuss what constitutes a member of the opposite sex. (It helps to demand a list of ten attributes.) When the list is drawn up, each group must rank order the traits in terms of what is most to what is least essential. Thus, #1 would be the trait lacking which a man is not a man or a woman is not a woman.

   Note: The exercise has been tried many times by various members of the design team. Men tend to be very physical and biological in their list and do a lot of hee-hawing while drawing it up. Women tend to include traits like "gentleness" and sensitivity," or at all events to give them high ratings. Women almost never consider a man's sexuality as his quintessence. Men usually give women's sex the highest ratings.

2. As the members of the class enter the room, hand out to them tags on which they write their first and last names. The men are directed to paste their tags onto their shirts, while the women hold theirs.

   The men are then asked to stand in a circle in the center of the room, while the women move about inspecting the men with an eye toward choosing a mate. When a woman finds a man she wants, she then writes "Mr." in front of her own name, and pastes this tag over the man's tag.

   The discussion afterwards about how the men felt, and whether women are still required to be passive and "wait" to be chosen, should be quite illuminating.

JOURNAL TOPICS

1. It is frequently said that one cannot love others without being able to love oneself. In what sense is "love" used here? Why does this love begin with the self?

2. Some say that the family is all washed up, that the institution--at least in our society--has outlived its usefulness. Others say that the family is needed to maintain whatever psychological and moral stability we have. What is your response to the family?

3. What qualities do you seek in a friend? As you look over the list, does it strike you that your "requirements" are self-oriented or not?

4. Are there any friendship groupings that the text fails to discuss?

5. Do you agree that Americans at least have difficulty with outward displays of close friendship? Do you touch, or enjoy being touched? Do you talk to your friends about how much you enjoy their company?

6. The text analyzes the treatment of sex roles in the films of Tracy and Hepburn and in the more contemporary *Kramer versus Kramer*. Describe the subject as handled in a newer film.

7. To what extent are you personally influenced by either the romantic or the Victorian models, as described in the text?

8. What is the range of roles that you play? Single out one role you are most comfortable with and one that you are least comfortable with.

9. Suppose you gave a party, and everyone you knew came to it. What "person" would you be?

MODULAR INTERIOR STRUCTURE

It is difficult to force a tight relationship between the two videotapes. One would surely not want to imply that love is *just* a matter of playing a role or that love is simply one of our roles. It is better either to let each program and the text chapter be what they are or to introduce a module by saying that love has many definitions, exists on many levels, and requires the assumption (which may be a better word than playing) of a number of different roles.

More important than a tight structure in this unit is *not* giving the impression that a really enlightened person is cool and cynical toward the idea of love. Fromm, after all, may be right; aloneness may be the one untenable condition of our lives.

The reason the subject was included in the course at all is that most students are going through a stage at which love is the major issue on the horizon. Interest in this module has always run very high. It tells the student that the course isn't just pretending to be--but really is--about his or her life. An introduction to the module which shows the student how sensitive the instructor is to this point should create an atmosphere of trust--and a willingness to listen with an open mind to the possibilities described.

ESSAY QUESTIONS

I. Text

1. Do you agree with Morton Hunt's sentiment that "love" is anything that makes sense to you when you use the phrase "falling in love"?

2. Suppose a person has just ended a close relationship, and confides to you "I was so wrong about love." Can you think of anything to reply?

3. Would society be better off if the family were dissolved as a sociological unit?

4. Mention and solve any two problems that family relationships can create.

5. What is a Platonic element in a relationship? Do you require such an element?

6. Is altruism natural to human beings? Does it have to be worked on? Is it possible at all?

II. Love: Myth And Mystery

1. What does an historical view of love seem to indicate?

2. If a society has no word for "love," are they missing something? Or may love truly not exist for some people?

3. Explain La Rochefoucauld's observation: "There are people who would never be in love if they had never heard of love." Do you agree?

4. What seems to be the moral of the story about blind young Pablo who falls in love with ugly Marianela?

5. Why was it said that Freudian psychology had a devastating impact on the romantic view of love?

III. Roles We Play

1. As used in the title of this film, what is a role?

2. Of the five central characters, which person seemed happiest and most comfortable with his or her life? Why?

3. Is it still true that people prefer having boys to having girls? Why, or why not?

4. For the most part, Greek women did not assume major roles in masculine society. Does this prove the Greeks were women-haters?

SURVEY 5 PRESCRIPTIONS

Answers

4 1. Each incorrect response receives the prescription:

Sophocles's Oedipus the King was composed about 430 B.C., and was immediately recognized as a great work of tragic art. Since that time, it has acquired the reputation of containing the world's most nearly perfect plot. Oedipus has long since killed his father and married his mother, without knowing he has done so. Sophocles's play is the tragedy of a man who must inevitably discover the terrible secret of his past and who cannot cope with the knowledge--a man who denies the truth, even when it confronts him.

3 2. Each incorrect response receives the prescription:

In the Glossary for Module IX of the Study Guide, you will find an illustration of a mandala, that most universal of all myth symbols. It is almost always circular, a geometric shape that most cultures seem to require in order to reassure themselves that the universe is one thing, governed by some unchanging principle, and comprehensible to their intelligence.

4 3. Those who responded #1 or #2 receive the prescription:

True, Oedipus was cited as the hero of a world myth, but King Arthur was also. Since the question asked "which . . . were," it should have been clear that more than one myth figure was involved in the answer. I recommend that you read the question stems carefully.

Those who responded #3 or #5 receive the prescription:

Captain Marvel was not mentioned in the text at all. As myth is described, Captain Marvel does not qualify. Like Superman, he is a flawless human being who is always successful in his fight against evil. Myth heroes can be of superhuman proportions, but they have human weaknesses as well. Oedipus and King Arthur were the correct answers.

Answers

5 4. Those who responded #1, 2, 3, or 4 receive the prescription:

Your answer is correct, but the most complete answer would have been option #5, which recognized that mystic numbers, journeys, and curses are all ingredients of myths. On an examination you may sometimes be asked to indicate the best or most complete response. Consider all possibilities before you answer.

1 5. Those who responded #2, 3, 4, or 5 receive the prescription:

There can be no question that space is the mythological frontier of our age. To have a mythology, we must have some uncertainties and some awe in the presence of forces beyond our ken. The soaring infinity of space provides modern mythmakers with endless possibilities.

3 6. Each incorrect response receives a prescription:

(1) From a close reading of earliest mythology, we can make a reasonable assumption that mythology developed from the need to explain creation, humanity, and death. To say that mythology is no longer relevant would be to imply that we now have a complete understanding of these subjects.

(2) How could early people have avoided myths, since all early societies developed a mythology, which they needed to help them explain creation, humanity, and death?

(4) Since a close analysis of earliest mythology reveals a preoccupation with questions of creation, death, and the whole nature of the human race, one cannot imagine that people will ever outgrow the need for myths. The big questions, after all, remain unanswered.

(5) Myths developed from the need to explain creation, humanity, and death. Many myths confront even the most tragic aspects of existence. They represent the attempt to account for them--not to deny or escape from them.

Answers

5 7. Those who responded #1, 2, 3, or 4 receive the prescription:

> The plots and characters of many Greek myths survive in the vocabulary of contemporary psychology. Not only do we speak of the Oedipus and the Electra complex, but we can analyze deep-rooted psychological motives behind extremely antisocial behavior as this is manifested in the myths. One thinks, for example, of the story of Medea--the mysterious witch whose magic potions helped Jason find the Golden Fleece, and who eventually murdered her own children out of a passionate, obsessive jealousy. Medea remains, thousands of years later, as a prototype of the psychotically jealous person.

3 8. Those who responded #1, 2, or 4 receive the prescription:

> Myths create models by which we organize our thoughts about ourselves and our universe. Mythology is not an alternative to science. Even scientists need myths. Nor does it make people feel of little importance in the universe--quite the opposite. Many myths confront the fact of death, accepting it without any certainty about an after-life.

Those who responded #5 receive the prescription:

> By projecting characters of often superhuman proportions, myths seem to support a faith in the human potential, but many myths end tragically, with the hero often destroying himself. Myths make existence comprehensible, but they are not exclusively "up" or optimistic. They give us models for organizing our understanding.

Those who were incorrect on this item but not on item 6 receive the prescription:

> Myths create models to help us organize our understanding of ourselves and our universe. I am surprised that you answered this question incorrectly, since you were quite right in question #6, which was very similar. If there was something in the wording of question #8 which confused you, I am sorry. Possibly I can improve the question in the future.

Answers

5 9. Those who responded #1, 2, 3, or 4 receive the prescription:

> In the world of myths, the hero almost always descends from a god. He usually encounters and conquers a wild beast such as the minotaur or a dragon. Like Theseus, he may lose favor with his people; or like Oedipus with the gods. His death is invariably mysterious, taking place far away. I can think of no myth in which the hero and his lost love are reunited just before death.

3 10. Those who responded #1, 2, 4, or 5 receive the prescription:

> This is the kind of information we derive from historians who studied the matter in much detail, and we either have to accept their findings or engage in our own research. When so many agree, however, I am willing to take their word for it that the tradition of romantic love can be traced back to the middle ages and the courtly code of relationships between men and women.

1 11. Those who responded #2, 4, or 5 receive the prescription:

> Options 2, 4, and 5 would not have been available to Ibsen as themes for a play. Birth control and planned parenthood were not issues in 1878, nor had women the right to vote. Whether the female actually defined and limited the male image would have been an irrelevant subject for Ibsen, who was overwhelmingly concerned with the theme of liberation. In this play he wanted to tell men and women alike that marriage should not mean the suppression of the wife's individuality.

Those who responded #3 receive the prescription:

> This error deserves special attention, for you recognized that this particular theme is involved in the play. However, it is the husband--not the playwright--who expresses the belief that a "husband's honor should be saved, even at the expense of his wife's."

Answers

4 12. Those who responded #1, 2, 3, or 5 receive the prescription:

> One could make a good case for the assertion that the very concept of family love--of caring for and sharing with one another, or making extreme sacrifices one for the other--may have originated with the early Hebraic tribes. Whether because of the religion, or the harshness of their lives and the strong need for pulling together for survival, or both, early Hebrew writings are filled with the sentiment that love for the family and the tribe is more important than concern for oneself.

2 13. Those who responded #1, 3, 4, or 5 receive the prescription:

> The Victorian model, delineated in the text chapter for this week, is that of a very traditional marriage in which the husband is supposed to be the strong, protective breadwinner and the wife submissive, or seemingly so. Thus, if a husband of today were accused of being Victorian, as this term is used in the module, he would have been doing or saying things expressing the belief that a woman's place is in the home. Another use of the word "Victorian" is in reference to a certain prudishness and sexual inhibition, but subsequent research into Victorian times indicates that quite the reverse was often true. But sex roles were nonetheless rigid and codified.

2 14. Those who responded #1, 3, 4, or 5 receive the prescription:

> Ricketts might well have thought his treatment of women was gallant, but perhaps some of his women did not. In any case, Steinbeck doesn't single out Rickett's gallantry or a concern for the preservation of the family, but rather, the man's love of himself in the sense of having confidence in his approach to life and being strong in his commitments. As used by Steinbeck, the term is exactly the opposite of selfishness.

Answers

1 15. Those who responded #2, 3, or 4 receive the prescription:

La Rochefoucauld, with his customary cynicism, is debunking the traditional notion of love as something profound, something spiritual. This statement implies that love is a matter of social custom for some people--he may even mean all people.

Those who responded #5 receive the prescription:

Your selection of this option has me puzzled. If you read the question stem carefully, and then looked at the options closely, you would have noted in option 1 that love is a cultural phenomenon and not a basic need--a restatement of La Rochefoucauld's observation. The odds often favor an "all of the above" or a "none of the above" option, but it is wiser to answer questions with knowledge, not hunches.

n/a 16. Each response receives a prescription:

(1) I think you could make a good case for this answer. One clue was the scene in which Nora hugs Claire's little girl as though she will never let her go. Another clue is the fact that Nora lies to the other woman at the reunion about her alleged domesticity, which may after all be something she secretly desires.

(2) I think you could make a good case for this answer. David's behavior is certainly not that of a man who is comfortable in a role-reversal situation. His macho tactics suggest he is trying to create a different image for himself, and in the concluding scene of the film he tells Nora he wants to find a job.

(3) I agree that Gail wants to look young and sexy, but she transforms herself into the flashy cheerleader for the reunion without much internal conflict. This tells me she is pretty conscious of her preferences and, of the characters in the film, was not the one with the least self-knowledge.

(4) I disagree with your assessment of Claire. The scenes between the two women suggest that, even though Claire is somewhat awed by Nora and afraid of speaking

up to her, she secretly pities her. In the reunion scene, Claire seems far more self-assured than Nora.

(5) This would be an unlikely right answer. All we really see of Tom is his effort to stay young, trim, and strong. He is jovially competitive with David, and no doubt enjoys winning the basketball match. On the whole, I'd say Tom is just fine, enjoys his life, and pretty much knows what he's all about.

1 17. Those who responded #2, 3, 4, or 5 receive the prescription:

When D. H. Lawrence wrote Lady Chatterley's Lover in the 1920's, British upper-class society was still very much under the influence of Victorian repressive sexual codes, which required that well-bred ladies and gentlemen must curb their sexual appetites at all times and never, never allow passions to become manifest, except within the very private confines of marital intimacy. Lawrence's novel about a lady's passionate longings for a gardener proved highly shocking and earned the author a somewhat sordid reputation.

n/a 18. Each response receives a prescription:

(1) St. Paul made a clear separation between flesh and spirit, and thus regarded physical union as being less than the union of souls, except within the sacrament of marriage. If you are not particularly religious, or are disposed to accept both sex and spiritual union as being essential in love, you may consider St. Paul's views harsh and, in this sense, cynical.

(2) Freud's theories strike the very romantic as being cynical, but Freud considered himself a scientist, not a poet. He thought he was being objective in postulating that what some called love is really delayed sexuality. Of course, recent critics contend that Freud has told us more about Freud than about ourselves.

(3) Perhaps romantic love is a myth dreamed up and accepted by romantics, but to call it cynical strikes me as being itself very cynical indeed.

(4) Eloise and Abelard were famous medieval lovers who entered holy orders after being tragically separated in secular life. Insofar as their own views of love can be inferred, they were perhaps cynical about those who did not or could not love--not about love itself, in any of its forms.

(5) This is the answer I would have selected. St. Paul was guided by a cosmic view of both the physical and the spiritual worlds and, in my opinion, can be considered cynical only by those who believe he should have thought as they do. Whatever private problems Freud may have had, he was a scientist and should be regarded as neither cynical nor otherwise. As for romantic lovers like Eloise and Abelard, one can only wish them all the happiness they can find. To love, even for a moment, cannot be construed as cynical.

1 19. Those who responded #2, 3, 4, or 5 receive the prescription:

Plato does not deny the pleasures afforded by physical union and its erotic sensations, but he does place this form of love on the lowest level of love experiences. He places agape, or the most intellectual form of love, at the top. Symbiosis is the term used by Fromm to refer to an unequal union between dominant and submissive types, while the other options have no direct relevance to the subject at hand.

3 20. Those who responded #1, 2, 4, or 5 receive the prescription:

The program "Myths: The Collective Dreams of Mankind" summarizes Carl Jung's theory that archetypes--characters, events, and symbols reappearing through different ages and cultures--have their source in a "collective unconscious," and embody universal human hopes and fears.

Answers

2 21. Those who responded #1, 3, 4, or 5 receive the prescription:

The Study Guide module "Themes in the Humanities: Myth," in order to show that modern people continue to measure up to the standards of the archetypal hero, makes a striking parallel between the life of John F. Kennedy and the plot of the monomyth.

2 22. Those who responded #1, 3, 4, or 5 receive the prescription:

A recurring human hope expressed in many myths is the return to a lost condition of freedom and abundance symbolized by the Garden of Eden. Many Europeans in the nineteenth century saw America as a chance for a new beginning in an unspoiled paradise. Mark Twain's character, Huckleberry Finn, believes that he has found that kind of life as he drifts down the river on the raft, constantly escaping the restrictive and corrupt societies settled along the shore.

1 23. Those who responded #2, 3, 4, or 5 receive the prescription:

In Plato's philosophy, the ideal love develops from knowing another's thoughts so intimately that a spiritual loveliness is revealed in them. What is known as Platonic love is love for abstract, intellectual beauty.

1 24. Those who responded #2, 3, 4, or 5 receive the prescription:

Attempting to understand the nature and meaning of love, the narrator recalls the love affair of the twelfth century philosopher, Peter Abelard, and his student, Eloise. They married, but the intervention of the church and the girl's parents forced them to separate. They both then dedicated their lives to the service of God. The question has been raised whether their love of God might not have been a sublimation of their sexual passions.

Answers

5 25. Those who responded #1, 2, 3, or 4 receive the prescription:

The point of the ballet is that a love relationship is often based on physical attractiveness. As you observed in the program, the handsome blind man is dancing with the young woman wearing the mask of a crone. Symbolically, his sight is restored, and he deserts his "love," believing that his true love must be his beautiful cousin.

4 26. Those who responded #1, 2, 3, or 5 receive the prescription:

It should be clear from watching the program that the "liberated" wife, while she may not rationally accept the delineation of women in her society, is not willing to be honest in front of a group of other women. It should be clear also that the husband has only pretended to be comfortable in the unfamiliar role of housekeeper. Playing the role only causes him to behave with intense "masculinity" in the presence of his male friends. The program is not advocating any particular role definition, but rather, honesty and realism in the role one accepts.

2 27. Those who responded #1, 3, 4, or 5 receive the prescription:

In recent years Freud's theories have drawn a considerable amount of criticism. The critics say, especially, that one cannot generalize about why certain people attract us and certain others do not. But Freud popularized the theory that the Oedipal conflict in the male, and the Electra conflict in the female, are never fully resolved in adolescence, and thus, when young people begin to search for a mate, they still unconsciously are seeking the characteristics of their mother or father.

3 28. Those who responded #1, 2, 4, or 5 receive the prescription:

St. Paul held that physical love, except between

married people, was sinful. He said that although it is better to remain single (for carnal desires impede spirituality), one who cannot control the passions ought to marry and remain faithful to one partner. St. Paul's attitude toward Eros, or physical love, comes from a drastic separation between the lower or animal self and the higher or spiritual self. The one is always the enemy of the other. In contrast, Platonic philosophy sees Eros as leading the lover upward to agape.

3 29. Those who responded #1, 2, 4, or 5 receive the prescription:

It would seem that the spaceman is most likely to figure prominently in modern myths, for space has become the new frontier, and represents for us what the mythmaker has always been drawn to: the quest, the garden, the unknown.

1 30. Those who responded #2, 3, 4, or 5 receive the prescription:

Donald Early states in his essay that our myths, more totally than any other source of information, can convey what it means to be human. Because they are universal, they reveal what is constant in human experience from age to age and culture to culture.

MODULE XI

THEMES IN THE HUMANITIES: HAPPINESS

TEACHING OVERVIEW

Happiness is of supreme importance to everyone, but few will agree on its meaning. Few recognize happiness by the same symptoms. As a matter of fact, a great many cannot even define what symptoms they are looking for. Often, in the absence of a positive experience of happiness, they suppose themselves to be unhappy.

The course design team believes that a humanities course should assist students in identifying at least the _kinds_ of happiness that can be talked about. The ability to analyze the nature of happiness coolly and intelligently before plunging into life experiences would prove to be a most valuable asset, creating reasonable and realistic expectations from life. That such an analysis is difficult and tentative at best should not deter us from the attempt.

The instructor should make clear that the module will neither exhaust the possibilities, nor reach a definite conclusion. Students will be responsible for a broad recognition of the range of options and some of the details of the major options considered. These major options are: hedonism, Epicureanism, Stoicism, the Aristotelian theory of happiness, and some of the concepts and assumptions people hold when they speak about idealism.

A workable alternative to teaching the material "straight" is to begin at the grass roots level, probing the attitudes--both certainties and confusions--which the class holds towards the subject. A simple question like "Who is happy?" and a simple directive like "Tell us what it's like" can spark a lively session.

CHECK LIST OF POINTS OR DISCUSSION TOPICS FROM TEXT

1. On hedonism - It is a common assumption that ours is a hedonistic society, but the issue is worth discussing. A poll of the class could bring to light some contrary data. We may be "closet" hedonists. It is doubtful that, if asked what their primary goals were, average people would answer "A large estate, with a swimming pool" or "A huge amount of money."

2. Big earnings theory - Whether openly admitting to hedonism or not, many are acutely conscious of deserving more than they get. Discuss possible reasons for this belief, and how it relates to <u>un</u>happiness.

3. Epicurus versus the hedonists - Is absence of pain better than presence of pleasure?

4. Stoicism - Is it better to deny yourself something very pleasant, if later the absence of it is likely to cause much pain?

5. Aristotle's theory is that happiness is the purpose of life, and the purpose of the state is to promote the happiness of the citizen. All good things exist for the sake of happiness, but happiness exists for the sake of nothing beyond itself. Hence, happiness cannot be equal to anything that promotes it.

   You can be miserable at this very moment, and still be in the midst of a happy life!

6. A possible limitation of Aristotle's theory is the assumption that the personal achievement of the good life is all that matters. But, the text asks, what about those who dedicate their lives to a cause beyond their own? Are they not happy?

CHECK LIST OF POINTS OR DISCUSSION TOPICS FROM VIDEOTAPES

I. <u>In Search of Happiness</u>

A. Faust's pact with Mephistopheles - A tradeoff of hedonism for intellectualism (another possible species of, or road to happiness not considered in text).

B. Old Testament Psalm - Happiness consists of God's protectiveness, and an abundant earth (and the two were related).

Question: Can people, faced with the all-consuming task of making the earth bear fruit, have any view of happiness other than one which relates to a full larder?

Question: Are most of us made unhappy by fairly sophisticated wants? Are we counting our blessings enough?

C. Christian view - Vale of tears, where none may expect happiness. (Are Christians still here?)

D. Hedonic calculus of Bentham - Try seeing if it works with measurable pleasures suggested by class.

E. Marx - Happiness is work, not leisure. And relating oneself to the product of one's work. Factory workers shown here do not seem to be happy. Are they unhappy?

F. Merton writes of perfect joy.

Question: Is joy the same as happiness? Does joy lead to happiness? Can we be joyous without being happy?

G. Drugs (and alcohol, etc., etc.) as roads to happiness through escape--or so their advocates believe.

Question: May happiness consist of not confronting unpleasantness? Are there times when not escaping makes little sense?

H. Faust's final realization - Happiness is a continual response to the challenges of life. It consists of the adventure itself--not of a tangible product, or the attainment of a goal.

II. The Pursuit Of The Ideal

A. If it is true that humankind is the only species that can be aware of being unhappy, may not idealism be a developed _natural_ tendency--a natural compensation?

B. More's _Utopia_ - Actually a satire on a corrupt England.

C. Plato's _Republic_ - A meritocracy.

Question: In a meritocracy, who is happy? Only those with merit? Or must those who remain "in their proper place" recognize that their lot is a happy one--even if it doesn't seem so?

Question: Does the prevailing reward system favor the meritorious? The nonmeritorious? Is it a random thing?

D. Thoreau - Happiness through dropping-out. Still a possibility?

E. Skinner's _Walden Two_ - A happy state is an efficient state.

Question: Can we be certain that a well-programmed person would not be happy? How would it be to live in a society relatively free from crime and violence--one in which people were thoughtful and altruistic? Does it matter if such conditions meant the absence of free will?

TEACHING ALTERNATIVES

If one or the other videotape is not shown, thus giving the instructor an extra day for class, an exciting session can result from the sharing of research data about the following:

Whether the majority of persons interviewed think they are happy;
What constitutes happiness, in their estimation;
What makes them unhappy;
How they feel about their work, or lack of work;

Whether they are working for something,
  or not;
Whether they are cynical or optimistic
  about improvements in the general
  quality of human life.

On the first day of the module, the class can decide which questions they want to ask, perhaps working out a point system so that each interviewee can be given a "Happiness Coefficient."

JOURNAL TOPICS

1. Do you accept the hedonistic definition of pleasure as being strictly sensory (physical) and strictly related to the experience of the moment? Or do you admit the possibility of other forms of pleasure?

2. How do you feel about the big earnings theory? Have you accumulated a certain amount of credit from life? Are you owed something?

3. The opposite of the big earnings theory would be a profound feeling of unworth. There must be people whose lives are clouded by the sense that they do <u>not</u> deserve any happiness whatever. What do you think accounts for this obstinate refusal to be happy?

4. Is it better to pick and choose your "spots" with care, so that you are never in a position to lose or to feel pain? Or better to take what comes without worrying about losing?

5. Stoics believe that "it's all in the attitude"--that all calamities happen inside the mind, rather than outside on the street, so to speak. Do you agree with this? Or is a disaster really a disaster, no matter what a Stoic may say?

6. Aristotle taught that happiness was the purpose of living, but at the same time happiness was not directly, not physically experienced like pleasure. Is this your idea of the purpose of living?

7. There are people for whom happiness is having and living by principles. But often, to live by your principles means to experience the scorn, even the hostility, of certain others.

How do you feel about principles? Are you willing to compromise at a moment's notice? Often? Infrequently? Never? Explain.

MODULAR INTERIOR STRUCTURE

In Search of Happiness presents an overview of the subject, while *Pursuit of the Ideal* presents a specific kind of happiness (idealism) which works for some, but not for others. The text chapter goes methodically from category to category.

The organization of the text chapter is recommended as a way of incorporating all of the module elements, for it presents major theories--and then possible criticisms of them. While the text does not deal with idealism, the subject of the second video program, it can be approached in the same fashion.

ESSAY QUESTIONS

1. *Text*

    1. Why do television commercials seem to assume happiness is for most people?
    2. Explain the big earnings theory as the basis for much unhappiness.
    3. Is the absence of pain better than the presence of pleasure?
    4. Is the party "before" worth the morning "after"?
    5. How would each of the following characteristically react to legislation banning the driving of automobiles on weekends: a Stoic? an Epicurean? a hedonist?
    6. How would an Aristotelian respond to the question "How do you know when you're happy?"

II. In Search Of Happiness

1. Using any system of hedonic calculus figurations, work out a mathematical score for going out to a party the night before an exam.

2. In the Declaration of Independence occur the famous words "pursuit of happiness." What do you think the authors had in mind?

3. Erich Fromm believes Americans are fundamentally unhappy. Do you agree with him? Why, or why not?

4. Is it important for a worker's happiness to have some relationship with the product of his labor? Or is a job a job?

III. The Pursuit Of The Ideal

1. What does a rodeo cowboy have to do with the subject matter of this film?

2. Plato's *Republic* was a meritocracy in which the brightest people had the good jobs and the important status. Would you be happy if all institutions were founded on the principle of rewarding merit alone?

3. B. F. Skinner implies in *Walden Two* that future societies cannot be allowed random development--that sound behavioral technology is essential. Do you agree?

4. As illustrated in the film, the Japanese in particular have (or at least traditionally have had) a serene, beautiful way of going about the simplest activities. Are there any "Japanese elements" in your own life?

MODULE XII

THEMES IN THE HUMANITIES: COPING WITH DEATH

TEACHING OVERVIEW

The course design team was considering for this module a title that is a question, but we were afraid that "What is Death?" might be considered facetious by the academic community. At the same time, however, that question is not really inappropriate to the approach taken.

This module recognizes that death is more than the physical termination of a given biological system, although it is probably *this* form of death that the average person fears the most. Attention is, of course, given to this fear--the sort of attention which until recently would have been distinctly out of place in a humanities course. The first of the videotapes, *For Everything, A Season*, looks at some reasons for this fear and concludes with some details about current research into the act of dying--especially the indications that it may not be quite the dreaded experience we hate thinking about.

But death itself is not one of the humanities--*resurrection* *is*. If the humanities are to help nourish the spirit, uplifting it when it is down, then death must be confronted before alternatives to death are sighted. Of course, we're not talking only about the physical act of dying, but also of those other forms of death: self-negation, resistance to aging, fear of failure, inability to face loss, and so on. The underlying premise of the module is that nobody owes life more than one death, but for too many, death occurs over and over again.

Humankind has ever been resourceful, however. Humankind has envisioned the means of transcending death. There are religious means, which need little introduction. But there are also so-called "Phoenix models," accessible to each of us, as well as to whole societies: urban renewal projects; Detroit's Renaissance Center; what San Antonio has done to its riverfront; and for the individual, altered consciousness, a change of life-style, self-forgiveness rituals. The second videotape, Phoenix and Finnegan, explores how James Joyce pulled himself out of a self-made grave of doubt and despair and, in Finnegan's Wake, conceived a life-affirming myth of human indestructibility.

Pilot test classes reported a broad range of reactions to this module. Some young people, of course, find death so abstract that they have no real fear of it--at least, not a conscious fear. Older students both recoil from and eagerly seek confrontations with the material. But even those who said initially that death was of little interest to them as an issue often become deeply involved in that aspect of the subject which delves into alternate forms of death, and into the Phoenix models.

In any event, we are living in times which, for many reasons, make a concern for death attitudes and life-affirmation meaningful and valuable to the college student. If nothing else, this module can offer the students some "reserve" insights upon which they may draw in succeeding years.

CHECK LIST OF POINTS OR DISCUSSION TOPIC FROM TEXT

1. Death and the self - In western society surely, with its veneration of selfhood and uniqueness, death has traditionally been the bane of human existence.

2. A Socratic alternative - In his final days, as reported by Plato, Socrates seems to have dealt with issues--not personal feelings. Upon his death, Phaedo realizes he is weeping for his own loss. Where truth matters most, death matters less.

3. In Buddhism, death is merely another phenomenon--not a dread event.

4. Glorious death, including honorable death in battle, and martyrdom. (Have we lost the concept?)

5. The idea of an afterlife comforts many. How strong is it? Strong enough to counteract the death-denying aspects of a materialistic society?

6. Relationships with the dying in our society (Kübler-Ross).

7. Symbolic murder and symbolic suicide as alternate (unnecessary) forms of death.

8. Priority listing - A mental notation of which people in our lives should die in what order.

9. Phoenix models - The natural cycle; thinking cosmically; recycling one's life; the "forgiveness" ritual.

CHECK LIST OF POINTS OR DISCUSSION TOPICS FROM VIDEOTAPES

I. For Everything, A Season

A. Images of the final moment. Death as the Grim Reaper. What other symbols of death continue to brood within the popular imagination?

B. Death as our cultural enemy. In a success-oriented society, death is ultimate failure.

C. The Pompeiian Principle - The sense that all of us are living at the foot of a volcano which may explode at any moment; the sense of everything "running downhill" (or, literally, out of gas!).

D. The Jazz Funeral - Are there any other such life-affirming rituals to mark death as a customary, not alarming, rite of passage?

E. Death - Town versus country. Is the pattern changing?

The living room wake versus the funeral home.

F. The bullfight as a life-affirming ritual.

Alternate view - That the bullfight is the acting out of an inhuman myth: man against beast; man superior to beast--in fact, to all of nature.

G. Gathering of testimony from thousands who have been close to death--the apparent universality of the experience.

II. Phoenix And Finnegan

NOTE: It is desirable to give the students some background on Joyce before they view this particular tape--especially his ambivalent attitude toward the Dublin Irish, his need for exile counterbalanced by his need to continually nurture his soul with Irish memories.

Furthermore, in order to fit the tape into the module, the instructor may want to explain before showing it that the title links the myth of the Phoenix bird and the resurrection myth of "Finnegan's Wake,"--which was an old barroom song Joyce heard continually in his youth, and from which he was to construct a mammoth work about the rise and fall and rise of humanity, represented in this film by the inhabitants of the pub.

A. The flashback technique used - Sequence following the teaser, when pubkeep welcomes the viewer into the pub, takes place in 1941. (Radio in background is giving news about the bombing of London.) In 1941, the wall is covered with Joyce memorabilia. Other sequences take place in 1900, when Joyce is a young man, or slightly later, when pubkeep is beginning to create the wall. There are some licenses taken--the Joyce who receives hate mail about _Finnegan_ is still the young man; nor has the pubkeep aged very much when he is aware of the existence of _Finnegan_.

B. What was Joyce's attitude toward the Irish?

1. They were braggarts, dreamers, hopeless romantics, incapable of seeing anything through to a conclusion.

2. They were, for all their rowdiness, sin-ridden and obsessed with guilt because of the dark shadow of Catholicism.

3. He resented them because he was one of them, and their problems were his.

C. From Dublin low life to a whole new style of literature.

1. There has to be a direct connection between the irrationality of the pub characters, who were to become so important on the pages of Joyce's fiction, and his structural and linguistic innovations.

2. In keeping with the theme of the module, the instructor might want to consider Joyce's departures from the grammatical mainstream as a Phoenix-type liberation.

3. Key line: "Don't try to make sense of it. But it sounds nice, doesn't it?" (Actual words from a letter by Joyce.) Creative spontaneity, trusting to instincts, as a Phoenix model.

TEACHING ALTERNATIVES

This module is so full of material that there is very little need to seek a variation of the lecture/discussion model. Once the ice is broken, once one goes beyond death-as-an-abstraction to the various death attitudes, students tend to open the flood-gates of curiosity and intense involvement.

There are, to be sure, "death exercises" which may be more appropriate for entire courses in Death and Dying. These include filling out one's own death certificate (wherein one discovers what kind of death he or she will or will not tolerate); writing one's own obituary, eulogy, or epitaph (wherein one discovers whether the attitude toward the self is death-like, or Phoenix-like); and demonstrating one's priority listing by arranging chairs, symbolic of one's intimates, in chronological order from birth to death, and then placing oneself in the chronology. (Definitely not recommended for general education classes in which students would have no expectations of this kind of exercise.)

A more productive exercise for general education--one more in keeping with the general thrust of the course--is to have the class members, individually or in groups, work out death and Phoenix models.

One could, for example, ask students to look through current newspapers and magazines for stories which illustrate symbolically either the death or resurrection of a person, an institution, a part of town, or a nation. If they discover a death model, their job is to suggest how it could be turned around into a Phoenix model.

If the class is already overburdened with homework, then one could devote part of a class period to having groups suggest ways in which an organization or an institution can die, and ways in which either can be reborn. An interesting variation is not only to locate death symptoms, but actually to name the cause of death (e.g., institutional hardening of the arteries, administrative concussion, poor circulation, etc.).

JOURNAL TOPICS

1. Supposedly Socrates was not concerned about his approaching death, but spent his final days talking about issues. Can you think of any issues which you regard as more important than your own problems?

2. How would a Buddhist explain what death is, if it cannot mean the termination of a self which does not exist?

3. The death of Elvis Presley drew a far greater national response than the death of Albert Einstein. What conclusions do you draw from this fact?

4. It is said that the way a nation buries its dead is indicative of its value system. What characterizes our method of burying the dead? What does this say about us?

5. When people say they are not afraid to fly, since when one's number is called it doesn't matter what one does, are they in your opinion exhibiting a death attitude, or life-affirmation?

6. One can tell a great deal about a society from the games its children play. The medieval "Ring Around the Rosy" was originally a plague-oriented chant. It is still being sung by children. Is it a death game? What about some other children's games?

7. Add some examples of symbolic suicide and symbolic murder to those mentioned in the text.

8. Do you observe any rules of age? Do you believe there are certain behaviors that are appropriate at a certain age, and not at another?

9. The text states that "the whole phenomenon of existence is Phoenix-oriented, not death-oriented." Does this include human society as well?

MODULAR INTERIOR STRUCTURE

This module deals with two kinds of death--one physical, the other symbolic. If one wants a tight structure, the simplest approach is to spend the first part of the week on physical death (and dying) as something generally feared in our culture; some of the reasons for; some of the symptoms of our death-denial (isolating the aged and the dying, and moving death out of the house); and some signs that people are becoming liberated from death fears.

The second part of the week can then be devoted to an enumeration and discussion of the various death attitudes (death models in everyday life), and some resources for life-affirmation (Phoenix models).

The two videotapes have an unmistakable yin/yang relationship with each other, but each also contains life and death models within itself.

ESSAY QUESTIONS

I. Text

1. On page 410 you will find a line of poetry by Emily

Dickinson. What does the poet mean when she says that death "kindly" stopped for her?

2. In your opinion, is it better to be straightforward in talking about death with children, or to idealize the subject so that they can handle it?

3. The text suggests that the Vietnam War witnessed a decline of "glorious death." Do you think "glorious death" is a concept for a nation to have?

4. Is it life-affirming to say that one ought to have as much fun as possible, because life is so short?

5. Why is compulsive gambling considered symbolic suicide? Do you agree? What about smoking and drinking?

6. Why do you think people are prone to symbolic murder?

7. If the depletion of energy sources is a death model, how can we turn it into a Phoenix model?

<u>For Everything, A Season</u>

1. The film suggests that the cosmetic industry is booming in our society because of a general fear of aging and dying. Do you agree with this assessment?

2. The film says that Pompeii is a symbol in Western society. A symbol of what?

3. Which makes more sense to you as a musical accompaniment to a funeral: a jazz band, or a slow hymn played on an organ? Explain your choice.

4. Do you think it is better to honor the dead in the living-room of their own house, or to use the services of professional funeral directors?

5. Do you accept the bullfight as a life-affirming ritual?

<u>Phoenix And Finnegan</u>

1. What use did Joyce make of the old drinking song about Tim Finnegan's wake?

2. How was Joyce able to turn the Irish, whom he considered rowdy and shiftless, into a symbol of human indestructibility?

3. The narrator of the film comments that it was humanity's very indefiniteness which proved to be the "saving grace" in the end of all. What does he mean by "saving grace"?

4. From your viewing of the film, what was your impression of the kind of literary style Joyce developed?

5. At the opening of the film, the narrator explains why the pub is a great institution in Ireland. Describe in your own words the life of the pub.

SURVEY 6 PRESCRIPTIONS

Answers

3 1. Each incorrect response receives a prescription:

(1) Intensity and duration are terms invented by the utilitarians in their attempts to be very scientific about the subject of pleasure. The Epicureans measure happiness by the absence of pain.

(2) The Utilitarians used the Hedonic calculus as a means of measuring the pleasurable consequences of actions. It was invented in the nineteenth century, long after Epicureans set forth the principle that happiness is measured by a sense of pain.

(4) The Utilitarians were concerned with the greatest good for the greatest number in their efforts to base a political party on the principle that the aim of government is to promote the happiness of the citizens. Epicureans measure happiness by the absence of pain.

(5) True, the Epicurean measures happiness by the absense of pain, rather than the presence of pleasure, but to my knowledge he makes no formal distinction between pleasure and happiness. He is happy having pleasure without pain. It was Aristotle who insisted on the distinction mentioned and said that, although pleasure may cause happiness, it is not in itself happiness.

4 2. Those who responded #1, 2, 3, or 5 receive the prescription:

Aristotle believed that the things which promote happiness can vary with the individual, but that happiness is the same for everyone. He believed that whatever makes us happy, we seek for the sake of the happiness--not for the things themselves. Hence, pleasure makes us happy; pleasure and happiness cannot be the same.

Answers

1 3. Those who responded #2, 3, 4, or 5 receive the prescription:

Epicurus was critical of the hedonists, not on moral grounds, certainly, but as a rejection of their logic. In his opinion, if one carried the hedonist's views to their logical extremes, the only means of attaining complete happiness would entail the experience of all possible pleasures. But one could never live long enough to experience all possible pleasures--hence, a hedonist must be continually frustrated at the thought of death.

4 4. Those who responded #1, 2, 3, or 5 receive the prescription:

The Utilitarians were the only group of philosophers ever to form an actual political party, and attempt to implement a powerful idea in binding legislation. This idea was that the purpose of government is to provide for the greatest good of the greatest number--in other words, for the happiness of the majority of citizens. One wonders whether any political party of the present could survive by its ideas alone, without making compromises for the sake of getting votes.

n/a 5. Each response receives a prescription:

(1) If this headline makes you happiest, then you are probably sympathetic with the philosophy of hedonism. But in these times, when energy sources are running out, one wonders how sensible self-indulgence can be anymore. A larger view may be all that will aid one's own survival chances in the long-run.

(2) You are evidently concerned about the national economy as a barometer of the national health; however, the Dow Jones average is peculiarly erratic and not all that rational. It can soar on the wings of remotely encouraging news, or go up simply in the absence of bad news. Dow Jones seldom thinks far ahead or worries about energy and environmental problems, unless these directly affect business prospects.

(3) Like many of us, you worry about world conditions. You find it difficult to enjoy your own personal comforts

when you think about misery and violence elsewhere. An enlarged sensibility is not the worst attribute you could have.

(4) You appear to have the interest of others at heart and are not narrowly preoccupied with self. Also, like many of us, you probably rejoice at any news which indicates a moral equivalent of war--a mobilization of resources in the interest of peace and the betterment of humankind.

(5) You appear to distrust the establishment so much that news of corruption delights, rather than angers or saddens, you. I have no doubt that a good many rather enjoyed the Watergate scandals on the grounds that their assessment of politicians had been justified. I would think it a sign of greater maturity for one to shake his head sadly at such a headline, and then proceed to act with personal integrity.

1 6. Those who responded #2, 3, 4, or 5 receive the prescription:

One cannot be certain that the little girl is consciously viewing the event of the bird's death in any definite way, but her actions and her attitude of unemotional calm strongly suggest that she is not uncomfortable with this death, and knows it has a rightful place. A theme that runs through the course is the child's intuitive grasp of such matters.

4 7. Each incorrect response receives a prescription:

(1) I take it that the image of the reeds in the river must have made an impression on you, but if you recall, the imagery was used to illustrate the Chinese philosopher Lao-Tzu's observation that the way of life is soft and the way of death is hard.

(2) There is much reverence and respect for the dead in Eastern society, but there is also very much more acceptance of the phenomenon of death. I doubt very much that the typical Eastern funeral is characterized by long eulogies.

(3) Certainly there are many people in the West who for one reason or another would be reserved, and show

little grief at a funeral, but since you were asked to select a statement of contrast, this option would have to imply that the reverse was true in the East--most unlikely.

(5) Like any large American city, New York generally puts death in its place--which is the funeral home. One doubts that the average child in New York has had an encounter with death before the age of five. Besides, "encounter" suggests conscious awareness. Death may not make a strong impression on any child that young.

3 8. Those who responded #1, 2, 4, or 5 receive the prescription:

Participants and musicians alike at New Orleans jazz funerals have expressed the opinion that the purpose of the lively music and the street dancing is to show joy that the departed is free from life's pain, and also is now in a far happier place. Other cultures have similar customs. In Puerto Rico, for example, people celebrate the death of a child under seven, believing that one who dies without sin is now sainted.

4 9. Those who responded #1, 2, 3, or 5 receive the prescription:

Tourists and people from outside the culture sometimes are shocked by bullfights, denouncing what they consider to be the inhuman practices. They cite, for example, the Picadors sticking many swords into the bull's neck--causing much bleeding--before the Matador goes in for the kill. Those who patiently explain the ritual, however, point out that every practice has its purpose, none of them inhumane. The drawing of blood keeps the bull from going blind. Of course, the whole idea of killing the bull is repugnant to those who do not try to understand the bullfight from the cultural viewpoint--who cannot see it as an embodiment of life's struggle against death.

2 10. Each incorrect response receives a prescription:

(1) The helping network, the support a grieving person

receives from friends, is very important but, if the survivor has needed the departed to reinforce his own identity, there is just so much comfort that others can give. A part of the survivor will have been lost, and the healing process can take years.

(3) Of course it helps the survivor to know that the departed has shown courage at the last--but the courage, after all, was not necessarily his own. If the survivor has needed the departed to reinforce his own identity, regardless of the manner in which death has been faced, a part of the survivor will have been lost, and the healing process can take years. Under these circumstances, the age of the departed will be of little consequence.

(4) Whether a survivor is or is not present at the moment of death may not matter if the survivor's frame of mind is negative. Such negativity is most likely to occur when the survivor has needed the departed as a reinforcement of his own identity, for this means that a part of him is lost.

(5) If the survivor has needed the departed to reinforce his own identity, a part of him will have been lost, and the healing process can take years. Under these circumstances, the age of the departed will be of little consequence.

1 11. Those who responded #2, 3, 4, or 5 receive the prescription:

This material was covered at the end of the film, "For Everything, A Season." "The Tibetan Book of the Dead" describes certain aspects of the dying process in ways that are remarkably similar to the out-of-body experiences of people brought back from the edge of life.

2 12. Those who responded #1, 3, 4, or 5 receive the prescription:

This famous soliloquy does not make a final statement about living or dying. Hamlet seems to be contemplating suicide and wonders why he should suffer "the slings and arrows of outrageous fortune," when he could so easily slip away and die. But he stops short of agreeing with this view. Death, he decides, is too much of an unknown quantity. It is "the undiscovered country from whose bourn no traveler returns . . ."

4 13. Those who responded #1, 2, 3, or 5 receive the prescription:

This is the kind of question that is not really difficult, but the wording of the stem can be tricky. You have to read the stem quite carefully, and make certain you know exactly what is says and what it asks for. You are looking for a statement of contrast, which means that the option statement and the opposite of it must be true. Of all the choices, only number 4 states a contrast: it says that rural people are more likely, and at an earlier age, to be accustomed to death. It seems a safe assumption that city people are not. There are many reasons for this, including the all-important fact that city people are more likely to make use of the funeral homes, thus delaying a young child's first encounter with death.

4 14. Those who responded #1, 2, 3, or 5 receive the prescription:

One can hardly imagine death's being feared because it is a release from suffering. Wouldn't the suffering itself be feared? When it comes to a painful illness for which there is no cure, death is often longed for by both the dying patient and the family.

3 15. Those who responded #1 or #2 receive the prescription:

Both the rank ordering of football teams and the selling of real estate for a profit represent part of the ongoing business of living. They neither affirm nor deny life. In what sense do they represent a rebirth after a bad period of depression or defeat? But completing a college degree at the age of 70, a time when most "senior citizens" are supposed to be watching the sand run out, would certainly be a Phoenix symbol.

Answers

Those who responded #4 receive the prescription:

Often the tearing down of old buildings and the erection of new ones would be definite Phoenix symbols, but in this case we have no information that the housing project is in bad shape, or that the shopping center is needed or will profit great numbers of people. But completing a college degree at an age when most "senior citizens" are supposed to be watching the sand run out would certainly constitute a Phoenix symbol.

Those who responded #5 receive the prescription:

Physical fitness is fine, but it can be indulged in anywhere, while cancer research cannot. Therefore, I cannot agree that this is a Phoenix symbol. But it is Phoenix-like for a 70 year old, whom society expects to be sitting around and watching the sand run out, to complete a college degree.

5 16. Those who responded #1, 2, 3, or 4 receive the prescription:

In the ballad "Finnegan's Wake," Tim Finnegan is a tipsy Irishman who dies in a fall from a ladder. At his wake, a fight breaks out and whiskey is spilled on the corpse, who then revives and jumps up from his bier--a comic counterpart to the Phoenix that is reborn from its ashes. Joyce's novel makes use of Tim's story to create a myth of the cyclical death and rebirth of humanity, which is personified in the rise, fall, and renewal of H. C. Earwicker.

4 17. Those who responded #1, 2, 3, or 5 receive the prescription:

At the end of Goethe's philosophical drama, Faust makes the statement quoted in the question. Mephistopheles, you will remember, is the cynical spirit permitted by God to test whether human goodness can endure repeated disillusionment and failure. Faust is a model of the good man who, through striving, God maintains, will achieve salvation in spite of his errors.

Answers

1 18. Those who responded #2, 3, 4, or 5 receive the prescription:

> Faust as a youth struggles to master the secrets of the universe in his quest for happiness. As an old man, he finds satisfaction in a practical though limited project--draining a swampland in hopes of rendering it fit for human use. Faust has come to realize that one can achieve happiness only by responding to continual challenges, whether one is ultimately successful or not.

1 19. Those who responded #2, 3, 4, or 5 receive the prescription:

> Egyptian mythology tells of the Phoenix, a bird said to live some five hundred years. It would periodically be consumed on a self-generated funeral pyre, be reborn from its ashes, and continue through the cycle of life, death, and rebirth. In the program "Phoenix and Finnegan," the Phoenix symbolizes the regenerative spirit of humanity--rebirth in a humanistic rather than in a theological sense.

1 20. Those who responded #2, 3, 4, or 5 receive the prescription:

> The term "Pompeian principle" contains a reference to the pleasure-oriented city destroyed in the eruption of Mount Vesuvius. In this module, the term refers to a particular death attitude--a hedonistic response to the fear that time is running out. The Pompeian principle says that since the end is near, one should "seize the day," live for the pleasures of the moment, and not be concerned about tomorrow. The point is made that while this is a frequent response today to the threat of worldwide disaster, it is not new, but reaches far back into our human past.

2 21. Those who responded #1, 3, 4, or 5 receive the prescription:

> Any one of these options is possible, plausible, and reasonable, but it is not the one Goethe provided for

his hero, Faust. The man's ultimate discovery is that life is a continual process; there is never any final product or total achievement, but an ongoing, day-by-day response to challenges. In the response lies the continual satisfaction. This material was dealt with in the video program "In Search of Happiness."

n/a 22. Each response receives a prescription:

(1) Some people are happiest and most assured of themselves when they are working for a worthy cause, even if they cannot be certain of success. I would think, however, that the true idealist believes his goals are practical. Often it is the non-idealist who observes the goals as being pipe dreams.

(2) Not every idealist regards happiness as an ongoing process rather than a definite product. Utopians tend to work toward a specific goal, something to show for their efforts. People who believe what this statement says tend to be more modest in their expectations than utopians are.

(3) Yes, I agree that utopians often rate principles higher than concrete reality. The fact that good principles are often refuted by what really happens seldom strikes a utopian as a valid reason for abandoning them.

(4) Though there is no definitely right or wrong answer to this question, this particular option would be my personal choice. I know I drive at the speed limit and try to avoid buying non-biodegradable products. I sincerely hope I'm rational, and to the extent that I can't sit back without doing my bit to improve things (however small that bit may be), I guess I'm a utopian too.

(5) This is a legitimate position, though it's hard to say utopianism is a fool's errand unless you've tried it a number of times and never had much success. This line of thinking is often adopted by those who have decided to be cynical beforehand and save themselves the anguish of failing. I think we all need to risk failure sometimes.

Answers

2 23. Those who responded #1, 3, 4, or 5 receive the prescription:

"Don Quixote" was originally intended as a satire on the medieval tale of chivalry which Cervantes considered totally outlandish. To poke fun at it, he invented the character of an old man who goes insane from reading too many tales and actually believes himself to be a gallant knight. As he delved into his novel, Cervantes deepened the character until Don Quixote became an almost tragic symbol of the deluded idealist.

3 24. Those who responded #1, 2, 4, or 5 receive the prescription:

If the Stoics believed people were free to change events in the world, they would have had no need of their philosophy, which advocates control of one's attitude toward whatever happens outside.

1 25. Those who responded #2, 3, 4, or 5 receive the prescription:

Jeremy Bentham, a utilitarian philosopher, devised the hedonic calculus in order to make pleasure susceptible to precise and indisputable definition. The real point behind his efforts was to show that government could and should exist for the greatest good of the greatest number, and through the calculus one could determine exactly what that good was. His system, therefore, aimed at measuring the pleasurable--or logically, non-pleasurable--consequences of all acts.

4 26. Those who responded #1, 2, 3, or 5 receive the prescription:

The man in question seems to be a rodeo rider who has either once seen or longs to see the ideal horse. The dream of white horses is shown twice in the film, the second time as a way of introducing the poem, "Ride a Wild Horse."

Answers

2 27. Those who responded #1, 3, 4, or 5 receive the prescription:

> Don Quixote is a visionary who undertakes to conquer the evils of the world at the price of great pain to himself, and in the face of impossible odds. Unlike the practical-minded Sancho Panza, he will not compromise with imperfection. To be called Quixotic then would mean that someone thinks you are an impractical idealist.

MODULE XIII

APOLLO AND DIONYSUS

TEACHING OVERVIEW

This is probably the easiest unit in the entire course to present to students. The subject matter and both films fall into a natural yin/yang pattern, one that strikes the students as quite real and, in many cases, a stimulating experience in self-discovery. Pilot test instructors were unanimous in reporting very exciting classes throughout this week of the program.

Both text and films place Apollo and Dionysus very briefly in their mythological context, and then move immediately into many manifestations of these two components of human existence. There seems to be no end to the number of applications that can be made, but apparently the greatest involvement on the students' part has developed from considerations of whether we as a society are currently moving in an Apollonian or Dionysian direction.

The Modular Interior Structure section will be omitted this time, since the subject not only suggests but represents a polar approach to understanding human beings. Thus, the structure is quite clear to the students.

CHECK LIST OF POINTS OR DISCUSSION TOPICS FROM TEXT

1. Nietzsche's original use of the Apollo/Dionysus dichotomy

sprang from his long essay on tragedy, and his contention that it was limiting to see only its rational and moral (Apollonian) elements. We should surrender to the passions of tragedy, the Dionysian elements.

2. Walking in a forest is a different experience for Apollonians and Dionysians. (One can substitute other experiences: dinner, movie-going, church-going, dancing, etc.)

3. The story and character of Zorba the Greek are worth spending time on, since the novel is actually about the clash between Apollo and Dionysus. The latter, of course, wins--and students enjoy discussing the wisdom or folly of the resolution.

4. The arts can be Dionysian in their assault on the emotions, but perhaps it can be argued that without underlying Apollonian control, art itself is lacking. Ravel's Bolero is a good case in point.

5. Rousseau wanted the arts to be revolutionary forces--that is, didactic, hence Apollonian. There are still those who insist that significance is the distinguishing characteristic of any work.

6. Education:

   a. Apollo as administrator. (Should Dionysus take over?)
   b. The Apollonian teacher has standards and memories of great student performances. Students need to rise to a certain level.
   c. The Dionysian teacher is non-threatening, willing to curve grades, willing to accommodate himself or herself to the latent potential in all students.
   d. What would an ideal course be like?

CHECK LIST OF POINTS OR DISCUSSION TOPICS FROM VIDEOTAPES

I. The Sunlit Chariot: The Apollonian Order In Human Life

A. The atomic model as a means of comprehending the workings of the universe has been subject to intense reconsideration in our time. Einstein, of course, firmly believed up to the last that he would be able to unite the microcosm and the macrocosm in one vast equation that eluded him. In addition, many continue to use the structure of the atom as a metaphor for a much grander organizational scheme. Humanists, in particular, need some Apollonian view of nature.

B. The A-bomb - Einstein recommended it first, then changed his mind.

Question: Would the world have been better off if atomic research had been discontinued?

C. Have we indeed lost an Apollonian control over the atom? (What about Three-Mile Island?)

D. Fra Lippi's work illustrates a nearly perfect balance of the Apollonian and the Dionysian in art.

E. Apollonian Protestant movement versus Dionysian Catholicism. Is this contrast still valid?

1. Protestant work ethic as an Apollonian discipline.

2. Is leisure Dionysian? And, do retired Apollonians fear too much leisure?

F. The Sacco/Vanzetti segment - Suggestion that Apollonian laws can be used for Dionysian purposes.

1. Possible tie-in here - Socrates' refusal to escape from prison, even though an unjust law had condemned him to death.

2. Point out Vanzetti's expressed belief that some (Apollonian) good would come out of the (Dionysian) tragedy.

G. <u>Lord Of The Flies</u>

Is the model accurate? Is humankind essentially Dionysian, held in check by an Apollonian surface that is skin deep?

H. Share with the class the poem by Housman, "The Laws of God, the Laws of Man," which concludes the film.

II. Dionysus: Ecstasy And Renewal

A. Main point to stress is that we derive a different view of Dionysus from this program.

1. Rebirth
2. Fresh ideas
3. Creative genius

B. The leader of the gang of boys on the beach is Dennis (for Dionysus). Note crown of seaweed which lands on his head.

C. Athens:

1. Rise to dominance of Olympian virtues--rationality and supreme physical discipline.

2. Less attention paid to Dionysian elements.

3. Coming of Dionysus (represented graphically in film) was literally the creation of a necessary balance, but Dionysians often went to extremes.

4. Gradual ascendancy of Dionysian domination, beginning in Hellenistic era (fourth century, on).

D. Medieval carnival (farewell to the flesh), and latter-day versions.

E. Apollonian Gilded Age (rationality of money and success) versus Dionysian anti-establishment Huck Finn.

F. Script author believes contemporary youth is Dionysian. Was this more the case in the late 60's?

TEACHING ALTERNATIVES

Text

An inevitable classroom exercise is to ask the Apollonians to sit on one side of the room, and the Dionysians to sit on the other.

Task: Each group is to draw up two lists, one containing the positive characteristics of themselves, the other containing the negative characteristics of their opponents. The lists should then be shared and compared in a community meeting. The lists should be about the same, except with positive and negative reversed.

What conclusions can be drawn?

Optional second task: Send the lists back to committee, so to speak, charging each side with developing a synthesis that would, in fact, be a composite of the ideal individual.

The Sunlit Chariot

1. Ask the students to bring in newspaper articles reporting events which illustrate an Apollo/Dionysus conflict. Have a sharing of reports, followed by a discussion of whether journalism tends to be pro-Apollo or pro-Dionysus in its viewpoints.

2. Have each person bring in a selection from magazines of ads selling extremely hedonistic products. Divide into small groups and analyze the material, coming up with an illustrated report on the Apollonian methods used to attract us into Dionysian extravagances.

Dionysus

1. A stereotype perpetuated through the centuries has been that men are essentially Apollonian, and women essentially Dionysian, in the way their minds operate.

   Task: Divide into small groups and ask each one to create a questionnaire, the answers to which will supply accurate data concerning the stereotype.

   The members of the groups can administer the questionnaires to each other.

2. An alternate version of the above exercise is to have the groups draw up a list of sources for the widely accepted belief that men are Apollonian and women, by nature, Dionysian (e.g., Adam/Eve; Samsom/Delilah; Rhett Butler/Scarlett O'Hara).

   In the discussion that follows, one might wish to try drawing some conclusions about the gender distribution of those godly characteristics.

JOURNAL TOPICS

1. Where do you find yourself at the moment in the seesaw conflict between the Apollonian and the Dionysian? Which side of yourself do you think needs work?

2. Some maintain that religion is essentially Dionysian because of its appeal to something in us that is not rational, and because of its frequent use of sensuous elements--music, large choruses, incense, etc. Would you agree?

3. Illustrate the Apollonian-to-Dionysian-to-Apollonian cycle in a particular movement in politics, education, fashion, or the arts.

4. Describe an extremely Apollonian class you have had, and an extremely Dionysian one. Which is more fondly remembered? Why?

5. Relate Apollo/Dionysus to two of the following: courtship; marriage; child rearing; organizations; competitive sports.

6. An extreme form of political Apollonianism is to place a product or service under a rigidly controlled national board. Should we nationalize any product or service in this country?

7. Presumably, the legal system is a model of Apollonian rationality and control. To be extremely Apollonian, our legal system would seldom bend. If it were extremely Dionysian, it would make many exceptions in light of circumstances. Which do you favor? Explain your choice.

ESSAY QUESTIONS

I. Text

1. Why did Nietzsche draw a distinction between the Apollonian and the Dionysian? What was he recommending?

2. Contrast the way Apollonians and Dionysians walk in a forest.

3. It has been suggested that rock is Dionysian and jazz is Apollonian. Do you agree?

4. Do you agree that love is Apollonian and sex Dionysian?

5. Are health food enthusiasts showing an Apollonian control over their bodies, or are they displaying a Dionysian addiction to a fad?

6. An ideal course should maintain a balance between Apollonian and Dionysian elements. Illustrate with specific examples of both.

II. The Sunlit Chariot

1. In the structure of the atom, what is Apollonian, and what is Dionysian?

2. What point, relative to the theme of the module, was made in the account of Einstein's efforts to stop the A-bomb project?

3. What point, relative to the theme of the module, was made by the reference to the Sacco and Vanzetti case?

4. What Apollonian elements in American life derive from the early Puritans?

5. What does Golding's Lord of the Flies have to do with two Greek gods?

6. The man shown walking down Bourbon Street blows out some candles before he does so. What is the significance of this action?

III. Dionysus

1. When the boys on the beach ruin the castle they have so carefully built, are they demonstrating a creative or a destructive act? Explain.

2. What effect on ancient Greece did the rise of Dionysian worship have?

3. Is there currently in our society a purely Dionysian movement? Describe it briefly. Do you think it will have desirable or destructive results?

4. Mardi Gras is one obvious contemporary version of the medieval carnival. Describe two others.

5. Huckleberry Finn, according to the film, came along as a needed Dionysian alternative to an increasingly conservative American society. In the late 60's, the film The Graduate had a similar function. Can you think of a Dionysian hero or heroine in a recent movie or television program that stands against a conservative establishment? Explain.

6. The film concludes with this observation: ". . . reason and light are always winning, but never win; and irrationality and instinct are always losing, but are never lost." Explain its meaning in your own words.

MODULE XIV

THEMES IN THE HUMANITIES: THE MEANING OF FREEDOM

TEACHING OVERVIEW

If instructor and class have made it to this module reasonably in one piece, one can move in almost any direction here. There is too much material to "cover," but by now the students should be into the rhythm of the course and know that the major ideas, not the minor ideas, are what count.

The main theme is right there in the title: What case can be made for or against the notion that human beings can (or want to) be free? If freedom to choose among significant options is a myth or a dream of humanists, then the whole point of the humanist lifestyle is amiss. So it makes good sense, at this late stage, to confront the big question of free will and expose the students to major detractors, the strong arguments in favor of a deterministic perspective.

The text chapter divides determinist thought into some (by no means all) of its important categories: Nietzsche's master and slave dichotomy; Marx; Freud; Skinner; sociobiology. Then it offers some possible alternatives, principal among them the humanist's answer to behaviorism--namely that one can, if one chooses, internalize the system of positive and negative reinforcements, liberating oneself (to a degree) from being totally a conditioned product. The existentialist position, which has been delineated elsewhere in the course, can also be reemphasized here. The Second Edition of the text adds a discussion of quantum physics, and its implications for the issue of free will.

The point is not to insist that freedom is a possibility, or even a reality. It is to remind the students just before they leave that there is no substitute for a conscious awareness of what they are about, and what is happening around them. If choices are limited, then what are the limiting forces? If legitimate options exist, what are they, and how does one get hold of them? This course has been about consciousness, and one may decide this is ultimately the same thing as freedom.

CHECK LIST OF POINTS OR DISCUSSION TOPICS FROM TEXT

1. One cannot repeat often enough the thought that freedom is not necessarily a natural condition, or a natural right. Whatever it is, the concept needs to be considered closely and carefully--not taken for granted.

2. The first major determinist argument considered is Rousseau's idea of the "Man with the Stick," the first exploiter, who made the institutions of society necessary.

   Question: Where did the Man with the Stick come from if the desire to exploit is not fundamental?

   Question: Must one be either the exploiter or the exploited?

   Question: Are the exploiters free? Are those who control the institutions free?

3. The next argument is Nietzsche's masters versus slaves.

   Masters value words like "power" and "achievement." Slaves value words like "kindness" and "sharing."

4. Dialectical materialism, or economic determinism, raises our consciousness about the degree to which money motivates our behavior. Communism, of course, is a political and social system predicated on the idea that the only way everyone can have enough is public ownership of all goods and property.

5. Classical capitalism may also be based on a deterministic philosophy, however. In the natural scheme of things, excellence must find its own level. Since not everyone can make it, those who can succeed should not be held back.

   Question: Once the capitalist system gets into high gear, can people freely enter it? Still, one continually reads of astonishing successes achieved by those who started out with little support and no capital.

6. Bureaucracy and freedom - (Though Proposition 13 affords a dramatic example of how the ordinary citizen can affect government practices.)

7. Character consistency - A frequently cited determinist argument. Are only mad people really free?

8. Freud - Our behavior is determined by unconscious drives.

9. Skinner - Our behavior is conditioned by positive and negative reinforcements.

10. Sociobiology - Our relationships with others are determined by genetic self-interest. None may perform an altruistic act which has no genetic "payoff."

11. Alternatives to determinism:

    a. Schopenhauer's idea of the will
    b. James's indeterminism - Since there is regret, there must have been an option.
    c. Quantum physics and the destruction of the Newtonian "perfect machine" universe, in which cause leads directly to effect.

CHECK LIST OF POINTS OR DISCUSSION TOPICS FROM VIDEOTAPES

I. A Cry Of Freedom

A. The boy's leaving home in opening of film illustrates what freedom means to great numbers of people: liberation from a bad scene--from a sense of being trapped. But is this the same as freedom?

B. Greeks seem not to have had the concept of freedom, but the life and death of Socrates perhaps suggests a true embodiment of the condition--the insistence upon one's moral and intellectual integrity, and the courage to accept the consequences.

C. Augustine tackled and defined freedom - A theological idea essential in accounting for human sinfulness and God's justification for punishing it.

D. Roger Bacon and the origins of scientific method - Freedom becomes intellectual liberation from superstition and ignorance.

Question: Have we lost--or did we ever really have--the idea that it is the mind which unlocks the door to freedom?

E. Duchess of Malfi - Literature and drama present us with the pageant of an engulfed humanity--almost never a liberated humanity.

Question: Is freedom always the thing we have just lost, or never had, or are prevented from attaining? Is it something defined by its absence?

F. Rousseau - A dream of the return to Eden where, in the state of nature, people are truly free.

Dream keeps recurring, even nowadays in the guise of Granola.

G. Cooper's Leatherstocking - The paradox is that people cannot stay in the wilderness indefinitely, nor can one be free in organized society. (Same theme as in Wright's "Man Who Lived Underground.")

H. Huck Finn as the all-American freedom fantasy - (But can you spend your life floating down the river?)

I. Were Socrates, Gandhi, and King really free people? If so, what conclusion do we draw? Intelligent compromise? Suppose compromise is impossible?

II. <u>On The Bus</u>

A. Possible meanings of the title:

1. The loss of choice; people who ride buses are at the mercy of the busline route, and the bus driver's whims.

2. Buses are "packaged" things--suggesting a loss of individuality.

3. Society itself, if it continues on its present course, may be riding a bus--to where? (Note that the young man who witnesses the execution of the last humanist decides he'd rather walk--so there is still time.)

B. The society depicted in the film resembles that of <u>1984</u>. What can we do to keep it from developing?

1. De-media-ize ourselves.

2. Read more; think more; listen more; talk less!

3. Bombard politicians with letters reflecting an in-depth knowledge of what they are doing.

C. Faceness and facelessness can become part of the class vocabulary.

1. When do we become faceless? (When we let those in charge make all the decisions, and never concern ourselves with what is going on.)

2. Why is the Grand Council faceless? (Because they are used to concealing their true thoughts and feelings.)

3. Who are the faceless people making news at the moment?

4. Describe a President "with a face." What difficulties would he or she confront?

TEACHING ALTERNATIVES

(Note: Group discussion topics can also double as Journal topics.)

The subject of freedom is so complex and many-shaded that the lecture/discussion method is usually rewarding enough without one's needing to try alternate strategies. However, the subject does lend itself to small group discussions. A good idea is to assign each group one aspect of the topic and end the week with a report on what conclusions were drawn.

Suggested group assignments:

1. Do people fall into the category either of Exploiter/ Exploited, or Masters/Slaves? Have they no other choice?

2. Marx was able to explain all events in terms of economic determinism. Can you come up with some examples that are clearly not economic in origin?

3. Determinists often cite character consistency as an indication of our lack of free will. Can your behavior be predictable and still be the result of free will?

4. Is Freud right--Does sexuality in one form or another underlie much of our behavior? Cite some examples that look as if it does, and some that could be used to refute Freudian theory.

5. Skinner defines freedom as liberation from negative reinforcements and dignity as the positive reinforcement of some particular achievement--otherwise, he believes these terms have no general or abstract relevance to the facts of human experience. Do they?

6. Sociobiologists analyze all human relationships in terms of genetic self-interest. Granted that "gene power" is very strong, and may explain some of our priorities, can we say that it explains all of them? What about people why say they have absolutely no interest in reproducing themselves? Are they "unnatural"?

7. Of the roads to freedom of will mentioned in the chapter--Schopenhauer, James, and self-imposed reinforcements--which, if any, offers the strongest argument against the determinist viewpoint?

MODULAR INTERIOR STRUCTURE

The text chapter, of course, divides handily into arguments against and arguments for free will. The first videotape, A Cry of Freedom, suggests that free will may be the costliest possession a human being can own--but may nonetheless represent the true basis for believing in human dignity. The second videotape, On the Bus, assumes that even if the humanist belief in dignity has valid roots, the world of tomorrow could see the end of the dream.

Thus, if one wants to tighten the structure for the week, one can use the theme of dignity--which is not inappropriate for a humanities course--and relate the text chapter's two views of freedom to this theme, climaxing everything with the second tape.

Although On the Bus was created as an allegory, each morning's headlines conspire to keep the concerns of that particular program quite current and, unfortunately, of continuing relevance. Dealing with the current world situation, in light of this program, is a distinct possibility for this week.

JOURNAL TOPICS

1. The text and the videotapes deal with numerous aspects of the term "freedom." Are there any significant other aspects which were left out of consideration?

2. Rousseau's famous position was that, if it were not for the oppressive limitations imposed by social institutions, people would be naturally good and benevolent toward each other. Can we do without government and laws? Can we do with fewer of each than we have? Who decides?

3. Do you consider yourself master-oriented, or slave-oriented? Or do you believe there are other options for you?

4. Assuming that many, if not all, of our actions are motivated by economic concerns, can we say that the communist principle of public ownership frees people from these concerns?

5. Many of Freud's theories are currently being challenged, including the idea that sexual partners are often parent substitutes. Do you think seeking a parent substitute is demeaning to dignity?

6. Humanists generally fear what they consider unfortunate consequences of Skinner's theories--especially the kind of society that is depicted in *On the Bus*. From what you have read about Skinner, do you believe he would approve such a society?

7. Sociobiologists like to point out that ours is a sexually permissive society because "genetic commitment" is no longer the problem it once was. Are there any reasons for sexual restraint, beyond genetic commitments?

8. At the end of *A Cry of Freedom*, we see the young man trying to hitch a ride to somewhere. It is easy enough to say he is not free at all, but perhaps an argument could be made for the contention that he is.

ESSAY QUESTIONS

I. Text

1. Rousseau believed people were born to be free, but recognized that for the mutual good each person must give up a certain measure of freedom. He thought people could reach a mutual agreement about it. No government has ever really allowed for it. Was he wrong?

2. Is it true that if you don't exploit others, somebody will exploit you?

3. How important is money in your view of things? Would you say it was the basis of your planning, and your way of relating to others?

4. Federal bureaucracy was cited as a major determining force in our society. Do you believe the private citizen is totally at its mercy?

5. What is meant by the observation that only mad people can be considered totally free?

6. According to Freud, are human beings life-affirming, or life-denying, in their behavior? Explain your choice.

7. If you were the president, and had to decide whether or not to sign a bill calling for federal funding of experimental behavioral engineering, would you do it? Why, or why not?

8. In your opinion, does it detract from the idea of mother love to say that a mother's altruism is motivated by genetic self-interest?

9. How does jogging help to suggest the possibility of free will?

II. A Cry Of Freedom

1. One historian of philosophy maintained that St. Augustine invented the idea of freedom "to take God off the hook." What could he possibly have meant?

2. Rousseau called for a return to nature--to humanity's natural condition. Do you believe humanity has a natural condition?

3. Would a Huck Finn, grown up, make a good president of the United States? Explain your answer.

4. By the end of the film, there is an implied distinction between freedom and liberation. Explain what it is.

III. On The Bus

1. The difference between humanists and non-humanists is shown symbolically by what device? What other device could also have been used?

2. Can humanism still make a difference? Suggest two ways it can or cannot make a difference.

3. The narrator describes his life-style. Briefly describe your own. Is it humanistic, or not?

4. You have just seen On the Bus and are required to take two positive steps immediately (however small) to prevent its vision of tomorrow from coming to pass. What would they be?

SURVEY 7 PRESCRIPTIONS

Answers

1 1. Those who responded #2, 3, 4, or 5 receive the prescription:

> Freud's theory of the mind (which holds that much of our behavior stems from unconscious and suppressed drives) allows for freedom of the will only in the most rational and balanced egos--while both Skinner and the sociobiologists agree that individual choices are determined by conditioning forces beyond the control of something we might call will. And the whole determinist school of thought (in which all actions can be traced to preceding causes) had its modern foundations in the Newtonian mechanistic view of the universe. Of the options given, only Schopenhauer's theory of will finds universal validity in the idea of personal freedom.

4 2. Each incorrect response receives a prescription:

(1) Apollonians--conscious planners and logicians--always try to steer the course of history in the proper direction, but history has a mind of its own. Apollonian movements tend to trigger Dionysian rebellions, which in turn inspire Apollonians to seize control, which in turn . . .

(2) Apollonians would like to think that Dionysian forces are inevitably overcome--but this is not the picture history usually shows. Apollonian movements tend to trigger Dionysian rebellions, which in turn inspire Apollonians to seize control, which in turn . . .

(3) As a matter of fact, there is seldom a time when Apollonian and Dionysian forces are in balance. Usually, there is a seesaw conflict between the two, with one dominant for a while and the other generating opposition--then the power positions are switched.

(5) Apollonians would like to think that they inevitably win out--that the Dionysian forces are inevitably overcome. But history shows a different story--namely,

that one or the other predominates, and nearly always triggers the opposition of the other.

3 3. Each incorrect response receives a prescription:

(1) Rote learning and memorization are rigid Apollonian strategies. Creative responses, sometimes called divergent learning, are Dionysian.

(2) Apollonian educators tend to be less innovative and more tradition-oriented than their Dionysian colleagues, who stress creative responses from students.

(4) There may be some institutions with primarily Dionysian administrators, but for the most part administration demands orderly planning--a distinctly Apollonian trait. The emphasis on creative responses in the classroom is the most clearly Dionysian of the options given.

(5) If anything, Apollonian instructors would give more exams. Dionysian educators, who seek to inspire creative responses in their students, often dispense with exams in favor of journals, and even personal diaries.

4 4. Those who responded #1, 2, 3, or 5 receive the prescription:

Western culture has always had an Apollonian bias when it comes to the manner in which we relate to the universe. It has long been an Apollonian dream that the universe will someday be totally understood by human reason. Instinct, feelings, and the pleasures of youth are Dionysian bywords.

5 5. Those who responded #1 receive the prescription:

This is not an unintelligent response to the question, for surely the current state of quantum physics is creating a picture of a universe which does not quite make sense in the old way human beings assumed. But it is inaccurate to make a sweeping generalization and say that quantum scientists absolutely hold out no hope for ever understanding the universe. If such were the case, why would they continue their speculations?

Those who responded #2, 3, and 4 receive the prescription:

Quantum physics, we can say at the moment, is changing the way we think about and relate to reality, however that may be defined. What makes quantum physics so exciting is that it is pioneer territory for the modern intellect. Anything is still possible within its realm. All we can be certain of right now is that the expectations governed by human logic may fall short of their mark. Either logic will have to alter the way it operates, or we may have to abandon logic as the principal mode by which we approach the business of understanding the universe.

1 6. Those who responded #2, 3, 4, or 5 receive the prescription:

Although a Dionysian banquet could include musical accompaniment, exotic herbs, vegetarian dishes, and a yin/yang diet, none of these elements is essential. What would make the occasion Dionysian is the excess of whatever was offered--hence, above all else, there would have to be an abundance of food. Please note that the stem of the question asked for a determination of that which is the likeliest element--not the only one present.

2 7. Those who responded #1, 3, 4, or 5 receive the prescription:

Clarity, order, reason, and control are all characteristics of the Apollonian approach to life which--we would admit--is essential to any endeavor requiring careful planning and organization. Spontaneity is, unfortunately perhaps, the missing ingredient. The problem is that dedicated Apollonians run the risk of losing their imagination, even their nerve, and refusing to try something new and untested.

Answers

2 8. Those who responded #1 receive the prescription:

> This option sounds quite typical of Nietzschean belief and, if you thought so, you were right. Nietzsche did indeed maintain that the ideal response to a tragedy was visceral (or passionate) rather than cerebral (or intellectual)--in other words, Dionysian rather than Apollonian. But note that the question calls for an undesirable response from Nietzsshe's point of view. Of the options given, only the second fills the bill--looking mainly for moral instruction. This, of course, would be strictly Apollonian.

Those who responded #3, 4, or 5 receive the prescription:

> Options 1, 3, and 4 sound typical of Nietzschean belief, but you need to slow down perhaps and read the question more carefully. You were asked to select the one response Nietzsche would find undesirable. This can only be "looking for moral instruction," which is Apollonian.

4 9. Each incorrect response receives a prescription:

(1) Formalism is a tip-off that we are dealing with an Apollonian feature. Jazz improvisations are Dionysian liberations from Apollonian musical control.

(2) I wouldn't want to enter a Dionysian-designed building. Architecture requires Apollonian know-how and planning. Jazz improvisations are Dionysian liberations from Apollonian musical control.

(3) If a painting has balance, it is essentially Apollonian; jazz improvisations are Dionysian liberations from Apollonian musical control.

(5) I wouldn't want to enter a Dionysian-designed cathedral. Actually, the Gothic cathedral was so scientifically and precisely engineered that it could stand up without mortar between the stones. Jazz improvisations are Dionysian liberations from Apollonian musical control.

Answers

2 10. Each incorrect response receives a prescription:

(1) New England Puritanism is often represented negatively in historical accounts, but "The Sunlit Chariot," on which alone the question is based, symbolizes the Puritans in an eloquently simple Apollonian light. The Sacco/Vanzetti case, involving what many regard as a gross miscarriage of justice, was the only option that can be called a tragic consequence of an Apollonian order (here, the legal system).

(3) Einstein was indeed cited in relation to what he regarded as an Apollonian-based tragedy--the building and dropping of the A-bomb. The equation itself for the conversion of mass and energy has little to do with Apollo and Dionysus, but the execution of Sacco and Vanzetti was cited in the program as a tragic consequence of an Apollonian order--in this case, the legal system.

(4) The Mardi Gras in New Orleans is a notable updating of the medieval carnival, a Dionysian outburst before the Apollonian austerities of Lent. Of the options offered, only the Sacco/Vanzetti case was cited as a tragic consequence of an Apollonian social order.

(5) To be sure, the violent death of children in "Lord of the Flies" can be considered tragic, but it was clearly the result of a Dionysian overthrow of the Apollonian social order the boys establish when they first find themselves marooned on the island. Of the options presented, only the Sacco/Vanzetti case was cited as a tragic consequence of an Apollonian social order--the legal system.

4 11. Each incorrect response receives a prescription:

(1) In the seasons, the order would be reversed. Winter is austere and Apollonian. Spring is the season for Dionysus, with its rebirth and renewal. But the moon launch was made possible by Apollonian planning and logic, while moonlight appeals to our Dionysian delight in sensory experience.

(2) The order would be reversed. The King was an Apollonian because of his rigid controls, while the Boston Tea Party was definitely a Dionysian outburst of angry emotion. But the moon launch was made possible by Apollonian planning and logic, while moonlight appeals to our Dionysian delight in sensory experience.

(3) The order would be reversed. Structure is always Apollonian, whereas pure energy, not held in check by something, has to be Dionysian. But the moon launch was made possible by Apollonian planning and logic, while moonlight appeals to our Dionysian delight in sensory experience.

(5) Both intuition and inspiration are Dionysian elements, so they cannot represent the correct response. The moon launch was made possible by Apollonian planning and logic, while moonlight appeals to our Dionysian delight in sensory experience.

4 12. Those who responded #1, 2, 3, or 5 receive the prescription:

Einstein was aware that atomic energy could produce a powerful bomb; in fact, when he urged a program of atomic research in this country, he believed that Nazi Germany had already begun research that could lead to an atomic bomb. However, before the bomb was dropped on Hiroshima and Nagasaki, he had come to fear the potential of atomic energy for worldwide destruction. He urged that the bomb be placed in the hands of a world government, and that atomic power be used as a constructive source of energy.

4 13. Those who responded #1, 2, 3, or 5 receive the prescription:

The faceless people in the program symbolize a society in which efficiency is the highest priority. That the central character has a face indicates that he is willing to risk feeling and showing emotion in response to the world around him.

Answers

2 14. Those who responded #1, 3, 4, or 5 receive the prescription:

Symbiosis, as the term is used by psychologist Erich Fromm, refers to either a master/slave or a slave/master relationship between people--it is irrelevant in this question. Hegel gave the term dialectic to his theory of how the mind works. Like other things in nature, he maintained, the mind seems to oscillate between poles and strives for a balance between them. In order to arrive at truth, the mind begins with a thesis--a belief that something is true. Then the thesis is contradicted by its opposite, the antithesis. But the mind rejects the possibility that opposites can both be true at the same time, and so it reaches a synthesis--a midpoint at which it accepts what is true in both.

3 15. Those who responded #1, 2, 4, or 5 receive the prescription:

Skinner maintained that humanity is never really "free." Everyone's behavior is to some extent conditioned by a reward and punishment system (positive and negative reinforcement). He believed that if everyone were conditioned by a controlling power to act in the best interests of society, rather than to make selfish choices, an ideal society could be achieved--one in which there would be no aggression, crime, or exploitation. With Skinner, this is an example of "intelligent conditioning."

4 16. Those who responded #1, 2, 3, or 5 receive the prescription:

Schopenhauer contended that such a thing as the will does exist, and that the evidence is present in all of nature. For instance, if a person decides to perform an action--say, raise his or her arm--and does so, the performance gives objective evidence that the will has acted. The raising of the arm is an "objectification" of the will.

Answers

4 17. Those who responded #1, 2, 3, or 5 receive the prescription:

> On the Bus is a fairly sophisticated title, and one needs some experience in listening or watching for symbols in order to understand it. If you will remember, whenever the bus is mentioned, the issue is personal freedom and individuality. When the narrator is finally made to ride the bus to his place of execution, he has in fact lost his freedom. Therefore, the best response is "the loss of personal freedom and individuality."

4 18. Those who responded #1, 2, 3, or 5 receive the prescription:

> Here is another interpretation question. This time, however, your options were limited. The film had nothing to do with mass transit. Since the bus always has negative connotations, it is unlikely that the symbol can suggest the humanist's openness to traveling for its own sake. While the dwindling of the earth's energy is a major theme of the film, the symbol of the bus is never used in connection with this theme. Whenever the bus is mentioned, the issue is personal freedom and individuality. When the narrator is finally made to ride the bus to his place of execution, he has in fact lost his freedom. But when the young guard refuses to ride the bus back home, he has made the decision to keep humanism alive, and fight for freedom.

3 19. Those who responded #1, 2, 4, or 5 receive the prescription:

> St. Augustine addressed the subject of human freedom in the matter of original sin--Adam's disobedience of God's command. The question was "If God is all-knowing and all-powerful, why did He not prevent Adam from sinning? Is He not responsible for Adam's fall?" St. Augustine's answer was that Adam was given freedom to choose, and that the responsibility of choosing wrong was his alone. St. Augustine's argument brings us to the intrinsic connection

between making choices and bearing the consequences for them. Although Julius Caesar lived at an earlier period than St. Augustine, freedom was not one of his concerns. All the others lived much later.

5 20. Those who responded #1, 2, 3, or 4 receive the prescription:

Mark Twain wrote Huckleberry Finn at a time when the free, pioneering spirit of America had disappeared under the pressure of a rigid Victorian social order. Huck, in his refusal to live under the oppressive codes of that society, represents the Dionysian spirit that seems to emerge whenever a counterforce is needed against an excessively Apollonian society.

2 21. Those who responded #1, 3, 4, or 5 receive the prescription:

Apollo was depicted in Greek mythology as driving the Chariot of the Sun across the sky, providing daylight after the darkness and chaos of night. Light has come to symbolize the intellectual conditions under which the Apollonian qualities dealt with in this program are made possible--rational thought, order, discipline, moderation, etc.

3 22. Those who responded #1, 2, 4, or 5 receive the prescription:

The opening scene, in which the boys construct and then without apparent motive destroy a sand castle, symbolizes the theme of the program--the cyclical alternation between Apollonian order and Dionysian chaos in the individual personality, and in society as a whole.

4 23. Those who responded #1, 2, 3, or 5 receive the prescription:

The point is made that freedom is an ideal realized by a rare few, like Socrates, Gandhi, and King--heroic individuals who made courageous moral choices and paid the price for them.

Answers

3 24. Those who responded #1, 2, 4, or 5 receive the prescription:

> The word "carnival" comes from the Latin phrase meaning "farewell to the flesh." It refers particularly to the period of Dionysian feasting and revelry that precedes the Apollonian discipline of fasting and penance in Lent.

3 25. Those who responded #1, 2, 4, or 5 receive the prescription:

> Except for the last humanist alive, the people depicted in On the Bus were either mindless robots or cowards who dared not risk their lives in the interest of curiosity, the open mind, the questioning intellect. Unless we nurture our curiosity, we leave ourselves vulnerable and victims of those who would do our thinking for us.

4 26. Those who responded #1, 2, 3, or 5 receive the prescription:

> The young man in the film, failing to get a ride in one direction, simply crosses the road and hitchhikes in the opposite direction--apparently indifferent to where his freedom will take him. The question raised is "Now that I'm supposedly free, what do I do next?"

1 27. Those who responded #2, 3, 4, or 5 receive the prescription:

> While all of the answers are applicable to Nietzsche's Ubermensch, the question calls for a neutral statement. All but the first involve a value judgment. The only neutral statement is that the Ubermensch persuades others to share his view of reality.

4 28. Those who responded #1, 2, 3, or 5 receive the prescription:

> Behaviorists believe that people do not make independent choices, but rather are influenced by

positive or negative reinforcement from others. The humanist would respond by citing people--artists, writers, philosophers, for instance--who have maintained their individuality, their integrity, despite negative reinforcement. Such "free" spirits are motivated by reinforcement that comes from within, not by society's sanctions.

n/a 29. Each response receives a prescription:

(1) If the President relies on providence for his safety, he is acknowledging that a power beyond himself is in control of his life. Such a power can direct not only that the spacecraft will or will not crash, but also that the President will make wise or unwise official decisions. If you share the President's conviction, then you probably believe that events are beyond human control, and that there is no such thing as chance. It is a determinist view.

(2) Castro would base his prediction on the Marxist theory that the overthrow of capitalism is inevitable, no matter what steps people take to preserve it. Marxist determinism is based on the theory that human beings are helpless in the face of vast economic forces beyond their control. If you believe that people are capable of affecting the economy, then Castro's statement would conflict with your position on free will.

(3) The suggestion that the government should assume the care of gifted children reveals a socialist orientation. In a socialist society, government control is essential. In order to prevail, socialism must exclude conflicting viewpoints for the stability of society. The statement implies that if the government should take charge of gifted children, the best minds could--and should--be conditioned to support the ideology of the state. No doubt, minds can be conditioned, as the Skinnerians and our own experiences verify; however, whether they should be conditioned is a humanistic concern. If you believe that people should be conditioned to act in the best interest of society, the Progressive Party's proposal

would coincide with your view; but if you believe that being human requires questioning, making independent choices, learning from past mistakes, and actively creating the world you live in, then such a proposal would surely conflict with your attitude toward free will and determinism.

(4) The convicted murderer has accepted responsibility for his action, and is willing to take the consequences. In refusing to blame circumstances for his predicament, he is exercising freedom--even though he is imprisoned. If you believe that people are never really free to make choices, but are inevitably influenced by social forces, heredity, or fate, then the murderer's decision would be at odds with your determinist view.

(5) Legalizing cocaine would mean that everyone would then be able to choose whether to use it, and would have to take responsibility for the effects of the choice. Even if the decision to use cocaine would harm no one but the user, the existentialist would ask "What if everyone were to make the same choice?" One must consider the effect on the whole community. If you share this existential attitude toward "doing your own thing," you would agree that being human means accepting both freedom and the burden of responsibility it imposes upon the individual.

1 30. Those who responded #2, 3, 4, or 5 receive the prescription:

In philosophy, libertarianism refers to the belief that freedom is a meaningful term, and that individuals do indeed have the power to make a choice among alternatives--a choice that is not predetermined by existing circumstances. Of the five options presented, only option 1--Newton's world picture--fails to support this belief. In the Newtonian universe, which can be likened to a perfectly operating machine, governed by the law of cause and effect, whatever happens can be traced back to an antecedent circumstance which makes the happening inevitable. Thus, a so-called "free" choice is really the effect of a cause which has already determined what it will be.

MODULE XV

THE HUMANITIES: AN ETERNAL QUEST FOR FORM

TEACHING OVERVIEW

The substance of this module used to be found during the second week of the telecourse, and the accompanying chapter was Chapter Two. Both telecourse managers and text-users reported considerable student difficulty with the material at so early a time. Consequently, the discussion of form has been placed at the very end of the course and the text. The chapter has been extensively revised to make it, hopefully, even more simple for the average student--and to give it a certain measure of climactic significance.

Though course and text are modular in nature, there does exist (as I pointed out in the preface to this document) the possibility of teaching both so that they "come" to something after all. The teacher who (like me) requires some sort of closure, can point out that the previous modules and chapters all deal in some way with the concept of _form_--and that a _humanistic life consists of searching for_, _finding_, _appreciating_, _criticizing_, _even abandoning_, _and then creating new forms_.

What do we mean here by form? Why, significant arrangement, of course. The entire text chapter rests on that fundamental definition, and it can be seen at once that the definition allows for a number of options:

1. divergent theories of what constitutes significance;
2. divergent theories of what constitutes an arrangement;
3. a discussion of whether the perception of form is entirely subjective; and,
4. if so, where do standards of taste come from;
5. the difference between classical and modern arrangements; and
6. how arrangements affect us (i.e., what esthetic experience is)

Form will always be elusive and difficult to present to general education students, but The Art of Being Human accepts the challenge nonetheless. Isn't it better to confront the problem, breaking it into palatable components, than to do what hosts of humanities teachers have been doing for a long time--talking about form without ever mentioning the word or, worse, talking about formal elements and simply assuming that everyone knows what they are?

A very feasible approach to this final module is to pose the picture of humanity as being unique in its need for arrangements that are somehow complete--the dropped second shoe, in other words. Nobody knows for sure why we are like that. As a matter of fact, not all of us are like that. Some people can sleep quite soundly and never concern themselves about an undropped shoe. But--and here is the big pitch of the humanists--those people may be missing something. A life lived among significant forms is apt to be one that will add some of its own before it is over. In the final analysis, isn't it the quest for form which will determine whether we'll be around much longer? We can engage in anti-form behavior--like blowing up the earth--or continue to seek an arrangement by which human beings can coexist in something that deserves to be called peace.

In the final analysis, isn't there a relationship that can be shown between the need to put a painting on a bare wall, and the unwillingness to let the earth be blown to bits?

CHECK LIST OF POINTS OR DISCUSSION TOPICS FROM TEXT

1. The humanities can be described as a record of the process by which human beings create form out of formlessness.

2. Form is defined as significant arrangement, and we acknowledge the many ambiguities encompassed by those two terms.

3. An arrangement can be said to be significant when it is complete, but there are a host of ways in which "complete" can be understood. A good discussion piece is a Zen painting, which is "complete" by virtue of its degree of emptiness.

4. The classical world, in particular, saw completeness in mathematical and geometric terms. (A stone lion on one side of an entrance demanded its counterpart on the other side.) The Golden Section remains a shining example of a mathematical principle of completeness.

5. A tricky aspect of the question of form revolves around beauty. What is the relationship of form to beauty? Does whatever is seen to have form also have beauty? The text takes a bold position on the matter, and it answers yes. Beauty exists in the experience of something's possessing

form or arrangement. Thus, the door is left open for the all-important question of whether beauty is objectively there in the arrangement--or occurs in the interaction of the beholder and the arrangement.

6. The argument that beauty has no objective status gains much support from the issue of cultural relativity. It is absurd to say that the long nose of many Romans is less beautiful than the smaller, upturned nose of Anglo-Saxons, or that Afro features lack the "classic" beauty of the Nordic face.

7. The objectivity/subjectivity debate has many implications when we get into the matter of taste. If we grant that such a thing as significant arrangement exists--however it may be defined, and however relative it may be--we are still a long way from saying that an objective tradition of forms exists. Yet, dare we deny such a thing?

8. Plato's theory of Forms is introduced as a specific, classical way of approaching the objectivity/subjectivity issue. If only the Forms (ideas) are ultimately real, if they exist independently of the mind, and if beauty is such a Form, then what is beautiful cannot depend upon the perceiver.

9. This chapter is structured in accordance with a yin/yang principle. There is this possibility--and there is that. The classical world was more objective in its approach to form. The modern world allows for more divergence. When you add it all up, you come to the conclusion that there is no end to the kinds of forms that human beings create and experience. But that, after all, is the ultimate lesson of the humanities--human beings are endlessly creative, and will never reach a point at which the "final form" is realized. The quest for form must never cease, either outside of or within oneself.

CHECKLIST OF POINTS OR DISCUSSION TOPICS FROM VIDEOTAPES

I. <u>The Wonder Of Form</u>

   A. The structure of the film itself as an example of form - beginning and ending with the sea, which symbolizes the unending vacillations of humanity.

   B. Early civilizations seemed to need massive and eternal

forms. Related to a deep-rooted insecurity? Where are we today? What about "small is beautiful"?

C. East and West - Early and continuing differences in the manner of coping with change.

D. Plato's theory of the Forms - A complete separation of domains--a changeless world of ideas, and a changing world of matter which did not matter.

1. Platonic idealism - an ongoing alternative to the way of the material world.

2. Whether we have ever heard of Plato or not, there is a Platonic side to our nature, for better or worse. Each of us, at least some of the time, is motivated by a preconceived notion of the perfect form of a person or a relationship.

E. The restlessness of the modern self - A natural outgrowth of the rootedness of the classical self. One works from the other--One dominates over the other at various times in our lives.

Question: Do we become more classical as we get older? If not, should we?

Question: Are children modern, and adults classical?

Question: Was the generation of the 70's more classical than that of the 60's?

II. The World Was All Before Them

A. Students have enjoyed trying to guess the identity (or at least the nature) of the narrator.

B. Henry Adams' "Chaos is the law of nature; order the dream of man" may have been astonishingly prophetic, considering the era in which those words were written, with its hopes vested in progress and faith in science. Increasingly, science is beginning to suspect that nature is random, erratic, and without purpose.

C. The narrator's main purpose is to review the possible definitions of humanity, and see which ones, if any, work. As to religion--does it elevate humanity, made in the image of God, or depress humanity, sinful and fallen, and unworthy of God's mercy?

D. Golding's Lord of the Flies sees the civilized façade and the animal beneath. Many have feared that the surface controls are very thin indeed, and that the animal will eventually take over--destroying the whole enterprise.

E. The narrator looks at human monumentality (perhaps human pretentiousness?), and observes how little the great endeavors have amounted to.

Question: Does the rise and fall idea really concern those who are living life close at hand? Cannot it be said that any individual life amounts to little in the larger view?

F. The narrator pays some tribute to the human myth-making faculty, especially the hero myth, but observes at the same time that the myths continually deny the animal behind the civilized mask.

G. The narrator takes time out to pay a genuine tribute to Einstein as a representative of the best that humanity can become--but then he is reminded of the abuses of atomic energy that followed.

H. The human preoccupation with death and, because of it, the fear of aging. The narrator is critical of both, but can it be said that this fear has its use?

I. He admits to being moved by "the artists among you" and the glimpses that the greatest have had into ultimate mysteries, but how many have died alone, tormented by their very genius--reaching, like Melville, almost to the heights, but never quite (in their own estimation) attaining them? Does anything great come from such audacious failures?

J. If the artists have spoken for human dignity, too many others allow themselves to be (or can't help themselves from being) trapped in dull work and other uninspired routines, or in causes and movements that often turn into nightmares.

K. Small wonder (one supposes) that Skinner and others are calling for a technology of behavior, but the narrator doubts this will work, because even the most carefully designed program would have a hard time nailing down this baffling, elusive species that . . .

L. . . . nonetheless will not stay down, will not remain in defeat, will fall to its knees only to stand again and, like Milton's Adam and Eve making their solitary way out of Eden, has the advantage of all possible directions and definitions. Hence, the narrator closes his report "without a final sentence." And so does this course.

TEACHING ALTERNATIVES

Text

Task: Divide the class into small groups, and ask each unit to list as many non-artistic arrangements as it can. The list can be divided into social, political, religious, etc., groupings. Then have each member of the group give input concerning the degree to which these forms add to or detract from the conduct of human life.

The purpose of the task is to come up with a community report that will enhance everyone's awareness of the human relationship to form as an ongoing characteristic of human life, and to demonstrate how many of our problems arise as a consequence of both the need for and the limitations of form.

Alternate task: Begin with a brief discussion of the non-artistic forms within which we function, both of those which hinder and those which advance our chances for happiness. Then divide the class into groups, asking each to discuss ways in which an involvement in the humanities can have practical applications in the everyday conduct of our lives. That is, how may a person who loves the arts be better equipped to cope with problems created by the "other" forms?

I. The Wonder Of Form

A. Divide the local area into sections; then divide the class into as many groups as there are sections. Charge each group with an analysis of its section, in terms of classicism and modernism. In other words, each group should make a report on notable classical and modern landmarks in that part of town.

B. Divide the class into small groups and give each group a set amount of time to prepare an improvised skit, showing the manner in which classicism and modernism operate within a family.

C. Divide the room into idealists and realists. If necessary, subdivide until manageable discussion groups are achieved. Charge the idealists with coming up with original and defensible reasons for following an idealistic course of life. Charge the realists with coming up with good reasons for _not_ being idealistic. Then let the fight begin!

II. The World Was All Before Them

A. An obvious task is to have small group discussions concerning the points of this final program, especially the identity of the narrator. Charge each group with including in its report a "definitive" statement concerning the tone of the program--is it pessimistic, or optimistic? Neither? How does the group think the program intends to make us feel after we have seen it?

B. Since the program is comprised of excerpts from all of those which have preceded it, the temptation is there--and should be heeded--to deal with it as a summary of the course. Small group discussions can center on the making of a statement about the course, and what the students believe they are expected to take away from it. The substance of the summary statement should come from the program.

MODULAR INTERIOR STRUCTURE

The two video programs work more closely in conjunction with the text chapter than is usually the case with the course. (Such "looseness" was deliberately planned so that either component could be used without the other, and the classroom instructor could feel free to show as many or as few videotapes as deemed desirable.) Hence, the use of both programs is highly recommended here. <u>The Wonder of Form</u> presents the student with an overview of the phenomenon of form-making itself, and paves the way for viewing <u>The World Was All Before Them</u> as an acceptance of human restlessness (the creative kind)--a continual searching for new forms, which the students will hopefully find deep within themselves.

JOURNAL TOPICS

1. The text compares esthetic experience to the feeling of health one experiences after a long illness. There are doubtless other definitions possible. Think of three, and discuss each one fully.

2. Describe three characteristics in you that can be called classical, and three that can be called modern. Do you ever experience a conflict between them? Which side of you tends to dominate?

3. Ever since Plato, people have argued over the question of how we know what we know. For example, you may believe you have learned how to recognize a tree because you have been told what "it" is--but how can you explain the fact that you recognize <u>all</u> kinds of trees as trees, trees that look in no

way like each other? Your knowledge of "treeness" couldn't possibly wait for you to have experienced every possible kind of tree.

4. How do you define physical beauty in another person? Is beauty comprised of individual components like lips and eyes? Is beauty a matter of the total arrangement of parts? Is it a certain totality that transcends the parts? Is it physical at all?

5. Is it possible to collect objects of art as art--without having any particular emotion towards them?

6. Give reasons for the contention that good and bad taste are not purely subjective matters.

7. Give reasons for the contention that good and bad taste are, at least to some extent, relative.

8. Should municipalities maintain boards of esthetic control to guard against "esthetic pollution"?

9. Which personal forms have influenced your life? Which would you most like to change? What are your chances of doing so?

10. The narrator of The World Was All Before Them pointed to the story of Adam and Eve, saying it contained one kernel of hope for the human race. What is the source of this hope?

ESSAY QUESTIONS

I. Text

1. A given culture can be defined, in the vocabulary of this chapter, as a "continuity of forms." Explain the phrase.

2. Should an intercultural comparison of forms ever be made? Should the forms of one culture be taken as the standard of civilization, while those of another are labeled "quaint" or "primitive"?

3. What are some current standards governing beauty in our society, in terms of both bodily elements and mode of dress?

4. If a monument or building is regarded as "no longer beautiful," should it be torn down and replaced with something in the current fashion?

5. Describe something extremely simple that you regard as beautiful.

6. Using the whiteness of cream, explain as simply as possible what Plato means by a Form.

7. Describe two kinds of actions you consider to represent bad taste. What is the basis of your evaluating them in this way?

II. The Wonder Of Form

1. "No wonder we are drawn to the sea, perhaps the only perfect form we shall ever know." So concludes The Wonder of Form. Briefly, why is the sea a perfect form?

2. Which of the following moments in The Wonder of Form touched you the most:

   a. the rapidly moving clouds;
   b. the lady seated at the piano;
   c. the cherry tree sequence;
   d. the two lovers strolling through the garden;
   e. the white ship's prow cutting the green water;
   f. the sunlight bouncing off the sails of the tall ship;
   g. another moment (state which)?

   In a few words, explain why you were touched.

3. Describe one trait in yourself that is classical, and one that is modern. Which one predominates?

III. The World Was All Before Them

1. Summarize the narrator's opinion of the human race.

2. What does the narrator mean when he says to human beings: "The endless tides are in your blood."?

3. According to the narrator, was the fall of Adam and Eve a tragic event, or not?

4. The narrator, seemingly impatient, asks humanity "Why do you sing?" What answer would you give to him?

SURVEY 8 PRESCRIPTIONS

Answers

2 1. Those who responded #1, 3, 4, or 5 receive the prescription:

> I suppose there are some people who can sleep soundly whether or not the second shoe ever falls, but certainly the vast majority of us cannot. A desire for completeness appears to be a universal trait among human beings--though the word can be defined in a variety of ways. Even those who appear to be content when things around them are left unfinished would probably confess to an inner feeling of uneasiness, and a secret desire to have somebody correct the situation.

2 2. Those who responded #1, 3, 4, or 5 receive the prescription:

> Properly speaking, the Platonic Forms are ideas or concepts like truth, beauty, and virtue--abstractions the philosopher believed were inside the mind at birth. But Joad's famous example of the whiteness of cream illustrates very well what Plato was talking about. Whiteness, in the example, can be called a Form because it can be contemplated apart from the things that are white. As Joad points out, if all white objects were suddenly to disappear from the earth, whiteness itself would not. Like the Forms of truth, beauty, and virtue, whiteness participates in material things, but those things are not the only source of our information about whiteness. It has an identity of its own, an existence apart from matter.

3 3. Those who responded #1, 2, 4, or 5 receive the prescription:

> Whether beauty exists "out there," independent of the perceiver, has long been debated in philosophical circles. Many hesitate to state flatly that the experience of the so-called "beautiful" has to be subjective. One reason is obvious--the cultural traditions of various peoples, in which there is widespread agreement over works of art and important

artists. However, such traditions do not constitute anything we can call scientific proof. The Golden Section, which appears to be found everywhere--both in the natural world and the world of art--may offer us a clue that at least some kinds of beauty do exist apart from subjective awareness.

4 4. Those who responded #1, 2, 3, or 5 receive the prescription:

A Zen painting, as your text points out, is characterized by much empty space and only a few brush strokes. Traditionally, the Zen artist will meditate for a long period, and then execute the painting very rapidly. The empty space is intended to serve as a continual reminder of the Void, the nothingness of essential reality which the meditator attempts to confront. Therefore, it is said that the emptiness in Zen painting is really the significant absence of meaningless objects.

1 5. Those who responded #2, 3, 4, or 5 receive the prescription:

Greek culture epitomizes classicism, which is characterized by structure, harmony, and properties. The quest for permanence certainly explains the nature of Greek art, and it was shared by all those touched by Greek civilization.

1 6. Those who responded #2, 3, 4, or 5 receive the prescription:

You will note that options 2 through 5 describe objects or events that might arouse an esthetic reaction. Only option 1--the feeling of health after a long illness--describes an inner state, which is what esthetic experience has to be, however we define it. But there are good reasons for making such a parallel. The esthetic response is always unasked for--it comes when we least expect it, and serves no purpose beyond itself. Similarly, who can quarrel with the feeling of health, or say that we desire it for any ulterior motive?

Answers

2 7. Those who responded #1, 3, 4, or 5 receive the prescription:

> Eastern philosophers may differ over the way reality is to be defined, and how we should approach the conduct of living--but they share a fundamental acceptance of change as the law of life. Whatever reality is, it is impermanent and presents many faces to us. The West has been characterized by a wide divergence of views concerning change--how important it is, or whether (as in Plato) it is a complete illusion.

1 8. Those who responded #2, 3, 4, or 5 receive the prescription:

> The Theory of the Leisure Class, written nearly a century ago by a Scandinavian economist studying American buying habits, still has much to say to us--among other things, that economic factors exert a strong influence in matters of taste. In other words, a person prefers this painting to that one because the former is the work of a major artist and the painting is well known to be very expensive. However much we might wish to debate some of Veblen's ideas, we cannot deny that expensiveness often lends a special aura to an object.

4 9. Those who responded #1, 2, 3, or 5 receive the prescription:

> The Program Wonder of Form makes a strong distinction between the classical and the modern self inside each of us. The modern side of us likes to experiment--to pull up anchor and be off to exciting new places--and is, in short, continually restless. The classical self, on the other hand, seeks permanence and identity. It dreams of home, especially if childhood is associated with a definite place, with many family observances and traditions.

Answers

2 10. Those who responded #1, 3, 4, or 5 receive the prescription:

> That "beauty is in the eye of the beholder" has become one of the standard cliches, but it would have been the last thing to occur to Plato on the subject. Platonism is founded on the premise that the great truths are universal and unchanging, and exist quite apart from the individual. The beautiful is one of the great truths. For Plato, beauty was either present in a person or object, or it was not. The existence of beauty was never a matter of debate or individual judgment.

3 11. Those who responded #1, 2, 4, or 5 receive the prescription:

> The narrator of *The World Was All Before Them* keeps sounding as if his "report" about the inhabitants of Earth is going to be dismally cynical. But in the final analysis, he is very guarded in his opinion. From his lofty vantage point, the past, present, and perhaps the future all seem to flow like a river--and he is aware of one overwhelming fact. Despite the many follies and tragic mistakes of a human race, somehow (no one quite knows why) it always manages to rebound, and to make a new beginning for itself. Thus, he must close "without a final sentence," for he cannot find a way to prophesy the doom of humanity.

2 12. Those who responded #1, 3, 4, or 5 receive the prescription:

> If you listened carefully to the narration of *Wonder of Form*, you heard over and over references to classical forms (which are sturdy, monumental, and created with an eye to permanence), and to modern forms (which tend to be less conventional, off-centered, and restless, always suggesting change). You also heard the narrator indicate that neither the classical nor the modern side in us ever clearly predominates. A life dedicated to tradition and permanence can become dull, and awaken within us longings for adventure and excitement,

but a life marked by unending change can awaken dreams of home and stability. Thus, in the terms created by the program, the sea would be a perfect form, since it combines both the eternal and the constantly changing.

1 13. Those who responded #2, 3, 4, or 5 receive the prescription:

The title of the final program comes from the closing lines of John Milton's Paradise Lost. The full passage, which describes the feelings of Adam and Eve as they leave the Garden they have lost because of their sin, is as follows:

"Some natural tears they dropped, but
  wiped them soon;
The world was all before them, where
  to choose
Their place of rest, and Providence
  their guide.
They, hand in hand, with wandering
  steps and slow,
Through Eden took their solitary way."

You will note that, despite the sorrow of losing their Paradise, Adam and Eve have the consolation of knowing they are now free to do anything they want with their lives. In this sense, they are symbolic of humanity itself, as this course views it.

3 14. Those who responded #1, 2, 4, or 5 receive the prescription:

Energy is what most modern works of art suggest, in sharp contrast with classical works, which for the most part suggest repose and tranquility, energy frozen for eternity.

2 15. Those who responded #1, 3, 4, or 5 receive the prescription:

Since you missed this question, one can only conclude either that you did not read the text section on the theory of the Forms, or that you were singularly unobservant when you did. Plato's use of "Form" is unique--it means an absolute, or eternal truth, such as beauty or goodness. In order to distinguish the word from the more general term "form" (which refers to those qualities which lend a sense of completeness to a work of art), tradition has established the practice of capitalizing the word when the specialized Platonic meaning is intended.

5 16. Those who responded #1, 2, 3, or 4 receive the prescription:

Let us restate the law of the Golden Section so that you will always remember it. It declares that the relationship between two sides of a plane figure (often a rectangle) are such that the shorter is to the longer what the longer is to the sum of the two. The ratio is 1 to 1.618. Of the options presented, 100' x 162' would come the closest to providing us with a Golden Rectangle.

5 17. Those who responded #1, 2, 3, or 4 receive the prescription:

The universality of esthetic experience should convince us that the capacity for esthetic response to something, or to someone, deserves to be called another sense with which we are born or which, when acquired, operates automatically like seeing or tasting. The text refers to it as the seventh sense, because parapsychology has done so much to show that extrasensory intuitions must now be included as the sixth sense.

APPENDIX

HERE, WITH INDICATED ANSWERS, IS A POSSIBLE REVIEW TEST FOR THOSE WHO HAVE TAKEN THE ENTIRE COURSE OF THE COMPLETE TEXT AND THIRTY VIDEO PROGRAMS. IT OFFERS A RANDOM SELECTION. NO ATTEMPT AT COMPLETENESS HAS BEEN MADE.

MULTIPLE CHOICE:

1. D Behaviorism, as defined by B. F. Skinner, has least in common with which of the following: (A) efficiency; (B) management; (C) reinforcement; (D) freedom; (E) conditioning.

2. E "Them" in The World Was All Before Them refers to: (A) Apollo and Dionysus; (B) Marx and Rousseau; (C) slaves and masters; (D) animals and asteroids; (E) Adam and Eve.

3. A In a state of nature, people are really free, according to: (A) Rousseau; (B) Nietzche; (C) General Booth; (D) Golding; (E) St. Theresa of Avila.

4. B The narrator, in The World Was All Before Them, attempts to define: (A) freedom; (B) human beings; (C) God; (D) the past; (E) the nature of art forms.

5. C The Man With a Stick was the first: (A) Noble Savage; (B) Superman; (C) property owner; (D) altruist; (E) literalist.

6. D The narrator, in The World Was All Before Them, concludes that: (A) earth will eventually be destroyed; (B) anti-intellectuals are happy; (C) things will surely work out for the best; (D) if there is hope for the future, children provide it; (E) death can be conquered through marble monuments.

7. E Charity and compassion, according to Nietzsche, are held in high esteem by: (A) goodness; (B) masters; (C) Apollonians; (D) adults; (E) slaves.

MULTIPLE CHOICE:

8. __A__ For Kierkegaard, the existential dilemma was represented by the choice made by: (A) Abraham; (B) Oedipus; (C) Electra; (D) J. S. Mill; (E) Red Ridinghood.

9. __C__ A strong element in modern works of art is: (A) balance; (B) repose; (C) energy; (D) idealism; (E) harmony.

10. __D__ A little girl burying a dead bird was shown on the screen as what sound accompanied in the background? (A) Beethoven's Emperor Concerto; (B) Have I Stayed Too Long at the Fair? (C) Neil Diamond singing; (D) To Everything--Turn, Turn, Turn--there is a season; (E) A narrator describing rural deaths.

11. __A__ The territorial imperative, according to Robert Ardrey, depends on: (A) the instinct for property; (B) the importance of altruism; (C) Euripidean irony; (D) the ability to regret a choice once made; (E) love of animals.

12. __D__ An ancient symbol of rebirth is called: (A) the Apollonia; (B) the Stoa; (C) the Womb; (D) the Phoenix; (E) the Sphinx.

13. __A__ Critical thinkers tend to be: (A) analytic; (B) Dionysian; (C) disagreeable; (D) impulsive; (E) unhappy.

14. __B__ Which of the following is <u>not</u> usually found in romantic literature: (A) a heroine who is dead at the end of the story; (B) marriage between good friends who are comfortable with each other's imperfections; (C) the idealizing of main characters; (D) struggle to reach what turns out to be unreachable; (E) lovers who take their love as serious and unique.

15. __E__ It has been said, "There are people who would never be in love if they had never heard of love." This means: (A) love is false; (B) love cannot be experienced by the deaf; (C) love is a basic instinct; (D) love is a social and cultural phenomenon; (E) in matters of love, people are changeable rather than true.

MULTIPLE CHOICE:

16. __D__ "Call that art? I got a six-year-old niece that could do just as good!" according to: (A) the Mime, in "Way of the Humanist"; (B) Rousseau in "Discourses on Inequality"; (C) a line in the program "For Everything a Season"; (D) Woodrow Tatlock; (E) the figuratist to a literal friend.

17. __C__ Myths may be defined as: (A) escapist fantasies; (B) nightmares; (C) collective dreams; (D) lies, popularly believed; (E) obsolete, primitive, and unknown in the contemporary world.

18. __A__ Linear medium, according to Marshall McLuhan, is: (A) print; (B) television; (C) music; (D) rapping one's knuckles; (E) radio.

19. __B__ Invented in the 1400's was the: (A) alphabet; (B) printing press; (C) atom; (D) wheel; (E) steam engine.

20. __A__ The fatal flaw for most Greek tragic heroes is: (A) pride; (B) envy; (C) excessive desire for money; (D) willingness to risk all for romantic love; (E) too much obedience to the gods.

TRUE OR FALSE

1. __F__ Typical modern fiction is likely to contain long, elaborate paragraphs of description.

2. __F__ Although they lived at different times, Plato and Skinner are basically the same in their view that human beings act in accordance with their inborn, inherited nature.

3. __T__ Tragedy, more than comedy, emphasizes feeling.

4. __T__ The Marxist is an economic determinist.

5. __T__ The sociobiologist emphasizes inborn genetic traits as determining human behavior.

TRUE OR FALSE:

6. __F__ Alfred Einstein and Henry Adams agreed that there is order in the universe, even though mankind may not yet understand it.

7. __T__ According to Freud, behavior is determined by unconscious causes for those people who have not undergone psychoanalysis.

8. __T__ Human self-definition, choice, and responsibility are characteristic of existentialism.

9. __F__ According to Plato, the "real world" and "actual world" mean basically the same, and may be used interchangeably.

10. __F__ The doctors told Edouard that he was responsible for his brother's death, in The Anguish of Abraham.

11. __T__ Amusement that undeserving people have good fortune is one of the characteristics of a comic approach toward life.

12. __F__ Any relationship without sexual connections is Platonic.

13. __F__ The Achilles Heel is another way of saying "maintain your individuality."

14. __T__ The ability to regret is, for William Jones, evidence of free will.

15. __F__ Quantum physics, Newton's contribution to thought, describes a mechanical universe.

ESSAY QUESTIONS:

1. What is the art of being human? Why is it called an art?

2. Of the figures studied in this course, actual or fictional, which one do you consider the most actualized human being, and which one the least?

3. Interpret this quote from Aldous Huxley: "After silence, that which comes nearest to expressing the inexpressible is music."

ESSAY QUESTIONS:

4. All things considered, is it better to be classical or modern in one's approach to life?

5. Bertrand Russell made this distinction: "Science is what we know. Philosophy is what we don't know." In a world dominated by science and technology, is there any room for "what we don't know"?

84 85 86 87 9 8 7 6 5 4 3 2 1